After the Shutdown

Part I

THE READJUSTMENT OF INDUSTRIAL WORKERS DISPLACED BY TWO PLANT SHUTDOWNS

BY

Ewan Clague

Director of Research
Community Council of Philadelphia

and

Walter J. Couper

Formerly Assistant Professor
Yale University

Part II

FORMER L. CANDEE WORKERS IN THE DEPRESSION

BY

E. Wight Bakke

Instructor in the Science of Society
Yale University

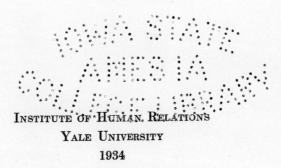

Institute of Human Relations
Yale University
1934

FOREWORD

As far as its resources will permit, the Institute of Human Relations supports research in biological and sociological fields, endeavoring particularly to create opportunities for coöperative investigation. A common ground for different but allied fields and a valuable stimulus for fundamental research can be found occasionally in the approach to questions of immediate and practical concern to the community. With this point of view, the Institute availed itself of a unique opportunity to observe the process by which employable industrial workers, suddenly thrown out of employment, endeavored to make a readjustment.

The study reported in this volume extended over a period of three years and was conducted as two separate, but related, investigations. The first part, directed by Messrs. Clague and Couper, followed the workers after the shutdown of the plants in which they had been employed for a period of eleven months when the opportunities for re-employment approximated those of normal periods., The second part, directed by Mr. Bakke, surveyed the process of readjustment during the two following, depression, years. In both parts of the study, the investigators had the advantage of counsel from an advisory committee consisting of a political scientist, an economist, a psychologist, an industrial engineer, and two sociologists. In addition to its intrinsic interest, the investigation has also served to illustrate further the importance of a perspective enlightened by expert knowledge in various fields in viewing complex problems of behavior.

MARK A. MAY,
Executive Secretary, Institute of Human Relations

iii

CONTENTS

PART I

THE READJUSTMENT OF INDUSTRIAL WORKERS DISPLACED BY TWO PLANT SHUTDOWNS

v

PART II

Former L. Candee Workers in the Depression

TABLES

IN THE TEXT, PART I

vii

CHARTS

PART I

xi

PART I

THE READJUSTMENT OF INDUSTRIAL WORKERS
DISPLACED BY TWO PLANT SHUTDOWNS

I. THE PROBLEM

A. THE SHUTDOWNS

On March 12, 1929, the L. Candee and Company of New Haven, Connecticut, a subsidiary of the United States Rubber Company, called a special meeting of its Factory Council, composed of plant executives and employe representatives. At this meeting the announcement was made that on April 6, 1929, the plant would be completely and permanently shut down. The L. Candee factory, in operation since 1842, was the oldest rubber manufacturing plant in the United States, the second oldest in the world. This announcement of its closing was the first intimation received by the plant officials and workers that any such drastic readjustment was contemplated, and it came therefore as a shock to all. It meant the displacement of about 800 workers who had thought themselves secure in their jobs for life.

The shutdown was made as the first step in a general program of consolidating scattered small plants into a few major factories. The New Haven shutdown was followed by the complete shutdown of the Hartford Rubber Works, another subsidiary, in late August of that year, then by two plants near Boston, and eventually by the shutdown of more than a dozen plants throughout the country. The closing of the Hartford plant displaced about 1400 men.

The shutdowns at New Haven and at Hartford provided an unusual opportunity to study the readjustment of displaced industrial workers. In each place a large group of workers, the operating force of an entire plant, were laid off simultaneously. One important feature of the shutdowns was that the Company paid a dismissal wage to certain of its long-service employes, which permitted the influence of such payments to be studied. Although this was not strictly the first, it was one of the most important examples of the use of this device in this country.[1]

[1] For discussion of the dismissal wage and related devices see Ross, Edward A., *The Social Trend*, New York, 1922, chap. 12; Vary, George W., *Special Retirement Adjustments*, American Management Assoc., General Management Series No. 89,

3

The conditions in New Haven and in Hartford in regard to personnel and plant, in regard to the action taken by the Company, and in regard to community response, differed in certain important characteristics, thus providing opportunity for comparative study. The Company offered the full use of its personnel records. Accordingly, the Institute of Human Relations of Yale University, at the instance of Walter J. Couper, then assistant professor of economics at Yale, and with the active and invaluable coöperation of Miss Eleanor Little, of the Industrial Relations Department of the United States Rubber Company, undertook to study, through a survey of the displaced individuals, the problems of their readjustment.

L. Candee and Company in New Haven was an antiquated plant for the manufacture of rubber footwear of various kinds. Much of the work was individual in character, little modified by mechanized or straight-line production. Some departments, such as shoemaking, consisted almost entirely of hand work. The workers, 60 per cent of whom were women, had become thoroughly adapted to these methods of operation, which made it possible for certain classes of workers to adjust their output to a short working day. This flexible working time was specially advantageous for married women, of whom there were many in the working force.

Long service was the rule rather than the exception in this plant. One hundred workers had been with the Company more than 15 years, on the basis of official records, while there were many who had served 30 and 40 years. The younger workers, with shorter service records, were in many cases blood relatives of the older ones, thus giving the working force a cohesiveness not wholly apparent in the service records themselves. Over 60 per cent of all workers in the plant were Italians, either foreign-born or first generation American-born. In one sense the plant formed a community in itself.

1929; *Lay-off and Its Prevention*, National Industrial Conference Board, 1930, p. 59, seq.; *Dismissal Compensation*, Industrial Relations Sec., Princeton University, 1931; Wolf, Harry D., *Management and Technological Unemployment* (In Schwenning, G. T., *Management Problems*, Chapel Hill, 1930); Myers, Robert J., *Occupational Readjustment of Displaced Skilled Workmen*, Jour. Pol. Econ., August, 1929. For a recent bibliography on the subject of the dismissal wage see G. T. Schwenning, *Dismissal Compensation: A List of References*, Monthly Labor Review, February, 1932.

Following the announcement of the shutdown the Company endeavored to facilitate the readjustment of the workers by means of certain remedial steps.

1. During the four weeks between the first notification and the final shutdown considerable latitude in plant discipline was accorded plant employes to assist them in applying for work elsewhere. The factory continued on a regular production schedule for cleaning-up purposes, but workers were allowed to be absent from work to make application for a job elsewhere or to quit without notice.

2. Arrangements were made to transfer employes to plants in other cities, particularly to the Naugatuck plant in a neighboring town. However only 35 workers, less than 5 per cent of the total number, were finally transferred. The policy of contraction which the Company was pursuing in their plants left little opportunity for new openings, and the workers themselves, because of family connections and property obligations, in many cases found it impracticable to move.

3. The Company's Employment Department made vigorous efforts by telephone, correspondence and interview to place workers with other firms. Special appeals were made to competing rubber companies and to plants in similar industries. These efforts were continued for some time after the shutdown, and altogether about 175, or somewhat less than one quarter of the displaced workers, were assisted in this way to find jobs.

4. Finally, for long-service workers, certain special arrangements were made. Superannuated workers, already eligible for pensions under the Company's existing pension plan, were retired from service; 51 workers received life pensions ranging from a minimum of $20 to a maximum of $80 a month. For the much larger number of long-service workers, not yet eligible for pensions, there was provided a dismissal wage of "one week's pay at current earnings for each year of service." This dismissal wage was given to, "1. All employes with 15 or more years' service not eligible for pension, and 2. All employes 45 years of age with 10 or more years of service."[1] Under this provision 116 employes, a little less than 15 per cent of the total, received

[1] Little, E. A., *United States Rubber Company's Use of a Dismissal Wage*, Personnel Series No. 6. American Management Association, New York, 1930.

payments ranging from $137 to $2,088 with a median of about
$400.

The shutdown of the Hartford Rubber Works, a tire manufacturing plant in Hartford, was conducted along somewhat similar lines. Announcement was made prior to the inventory
shutdown, about the middle of August, that the plant would
not re-open afterward. Pensions and dismissal wages were paid
on the same basis as in New Haven. The number eligible for
pension was very small, while 126 employes, or about 10 per
cent, received a dismissal wage.

The differences between the two shutdowns were of considerable importance. The Hartford factory produced automobile
tires instead of footwear. Its processes were more mechanized
and specialized. The managerial control was more taut. The
employes were practically all men, many of them single. There
were no outstanding nationalities, such as the Italians in New
Haven; and, although native second-generation Americans constituted the largest single group, they comprised only about one
quarter of the total. In addition, more effective means of enlist-
ing community coöperation were instituted than had been the
case in New Haven. The community was persuaded to coöperate actively in facilitating readjustment of the displaced workers; advertisements were placed in the papers asking the plants
to give priority to rubber workers in hiring; manufacturers themselves were personally solicited for job openings. The result was
a rather vigorous response for a period of from four to six weeks,
after which time the movement came to an abrupt end. This
was due to the sharp down-trend in business which heralded
the approach of a serious depression and which hampered the
placement of the Hartford rubber workers. The New Haven
plant had closed while business was still good and the workers
had some months of an active labor market in which to look for
work.

Here, then, was an opportunity to study under widely diverse
conditions two cases where large groups of workers were simultaneously laid off, to determine the means by which, and the
success with which they adjusted themselves and their families,
and to trace to some extent the influence upon that adjustment

of such factors as age, nationality, skill, dismissal wage, community efforts to assist readjustment, and the general employment condition in the industrial area.

B. Analysis of Workers in New Haven and Hartford

The differences existing between these two large groups of workers laid off under identical circumstances form the key to this study, because it is these differences which enable us to gauge the net effect of the shutdowns. Thus the results in one city could be used as a check on those in another. Because of the access to the personnel records granted by the Company, fairly complete data for each individual worker were available.

The first evidence that the differing situations in New Haven and Hartford might give rise to important differences in results came from the field survey. Over 92 per cent of the New Haven workers listed for survey were found and interviewed, while the corresponding figure for Hartford was only 48 per cent. This difference in coverage raises a number of questions. Was it due to fundamental differences between the working forces in the two plants? To what extent were local conditions a determining factor? What effect, if any, does this result have upon the problem of sampling, and hence upon the ultimate findings? Some analysis of this situation is a prerequisite to the presentation of the final results of the study.

The first question then concerns the comparison between the total working force in each city and the groups for which schedules were obtained in the field. The sex differences were insignificant. There were in the New Haven plant 265 men and 464 women available for survey,[1] of whom 244 men and 428 women were found and interviewed. The proportions were almost identical in the two cases. In Hartford schedules were obtained for 8 women out of 12 and for 526 men out of 1093. The proportion of women covered was higher but the number is so small that it makes no difference whatever in the total.

---

[1] The number of workers finally listed was 729 in New Haven and 1105 in Hartford. These figures differ from those previously cited because of the omission from the survey of two groups of workers (1) plant executives, minor officials and foremen, which the Company did not wish to have included, and (2) certain maintenance workers, such as mechanics and watchmen, who were kept on for some time after the shutdown and hence were not strictly comparable to the others.

There were, however, some important differences arising out of the age factor, especially in Hartford. The following table shows the coverage in each city on an age basis.

TABLE 1

Total Working Force, Classified by Age Groups, Showing Sample Obtained

Age Groups	NEW HAVEN		HARTFORD					
	Total Number on Force	Sched-ules	Total Number on Force	Sched-ules	Schedules Not Obtained			
					Moved Un-known Destina-tion	Unknown at Address	Moved Out of City	Miscel-laneous
Total	*729*	*672*	*1105*	*534*	*237*	*122*	*135*	*77*
15–19	115	103	20	11	3	1	4	1
20–24	111	99	151	46	53	19	27	6
25–29	113	105	203	80	61	25	24	13
30–34	77	71	201	91	39	28	29	14
35–39	71	66	199	109	43	14	19	14
40–44	76	70	160	88	19	15	20	18
45–49	57	52	83	50	9	11	7	6
50–54	34	33	36	26	4	3	2	1
55–59	34	33	25	14	3	4	2	2
60–64	28	27	17	13	1	0	1	2
65–69	12	12	9	6	1	2	0	0
70–74	1	1	1	0	1	0	0	0

Of the entire Hartford force, 135 were known to have moved out of the city, and it is probable that many of the 237 who had moved to an unknown destination actually did leave the city. It is also likely that many of the 122 "unknown at address" (often fictitious) were highly itinerant. When the address was not fictitious, they had at any rate not lived there long enough to become known in the neighborhood. In New Haven, on the other hand, many of the 57 workers not scheduled were definitely known to be still in the city.

The greater stability of the older workers in both plants is shown in the table. In New Haven the coverage for all groups was so high that the differences are not readily apparent, but the cumulation of a few age groups makes them clearer. For example, out of 108 workers of fifty years of age and over, only 3 were not found. On the other hand, in the three younger age groups, having approximately this same number of workers in each, the losses ranged from 8 to 12. But it is in Hartford that the effect of age was most evident. In the older groups the coverage was distinctly better than in the younger ones, especially in the two groups between the ages of 20 and 30, and to a lesser extent the group of the early 30's. The columns showing reasons for not obtaining schedules from these workers make it clear that these younger men were distinctly a mobile group; they had in most cases undoubtedly left the city. Hence the Hartford coverage of younger workers is less complete than for other groups.

One of the obvious reasons for this difference in mobility in the two cities is to be found in the sex composition of the working forces. Over 60 per cent of the New Haven workers were women and in the younger age groups women were in an overwhelming majority. The sex division in the Candee plant by age groups is shown in the table.

TABLE 2
Total Working Force Classified by Sex and Age
NEW HAVEN

Age Groups	Number of Workers		
	Total	Men	Women
Totals...	*729*	*265*	*464*
15–19..	115	27	88
20–24..	111	21	90
25–29..	113	27	86
30–34..	77	31	46
35–39..	71	26	45
40–44..	76	35	41
45–49..	57	35	22
50–54..	34	19	15
55–59..	34	18	16
60–64..	28	17	11
65–69..	12	8	4
70–74..	1	1	..

The young men in Hartford, being unattached, could move in search of work, while the young women in New Haven had to remain with their families. In New Haven, too, mobility was further reduced by the family composition of the working force. The Candee plant was distinctly a "family concern" in the sense that many married couples worked there, and that many of the younger workers were directly related to the elder. This family constitution of the working force decreased the mobility of the men, even the younger ones, and its effect upon the women is obvious. The point here is that age itself was not the most important factor in this situation; it was clearly nothing but an indicator of something else.

Nationality

Further analysis shows that the more important factor involved was that of nationality. Both these plants contained a great many foreign-born workers. In Hartford the working force was divided into foreign-born and native-born in the ratio of 56 per cent to 44 per cent; in New Haven the proportions were almost exactly reversed—45 per cent to 55 per cent. However, these figures do not give exactly the right picture of the situation. Many of these native-born were first generation only, the children of foreign-born immigrants. Living as they did with their own nationality group, and often speaking a foreign language, they were generally much more foreign than American in their thought and behavior. The fact that so many of them were young means also that they were as yet wholly under the control of their foreign-born parents. The next table shows the classification of the workers into the three groups: First, native-born of native parents; second, native-born of foreign-born parents; and third, foreign-born.

TABLE 3

Nativity of Working Force, Showing Schedules Obtained

NATIVITY	HARTFORD		NEW HAVEN	
	Total	Schedules	Total	Schedules
Totals............................	*1105*	*534*	*729*	*672*
Native-born of ⎰ White	275	131	61	51
Native Parentage ⎱ Colored	39	23	3	3
Native-born of Foreign Parentage	172	79	335	314
Foreign-born	619	301	330	304

The native-born of native parents (for simplicity termed "American" in the following discussion) constituted a considerably larger proportion of the total in Hartford than they did in New Haven. The native-born at the latter plant are shown to have been largely the children of foreign-born parents. Thus if these first-generation native-born are classed under their appropriate nationalities, it becomes evident that the Candee working force was composed very largely of various foreign nationalities. In Hartford, while the number of foreign-born was high, most of the native-born came of native parentage.

So far as the problem of coverage is concerned, nativity was of no importance. The proportion of native Americans surveyed in each city was approximately the same as that of the native-born of foreign parents, or even the foreign-born themselves. From a strictly statistical viewpoint, a better sample could hardly have been obtained had it been deliberately selected.

The next step in the analysis proved much more fruitful. All workers except Americans were classified according to nationality and birthplace. The results for Hartford are shown in the table:

TABLE 4

Nationality Groups, Excluding Americans, Classified by Birthplace, Showing Schedules Obtained

HARTFORD

Nationality	Total No. in Working Force			Schedules		
	Total	Foreign-born	Native-born	Total	Foreign-born	Native-born
Totals	*791*	*619*	*172*	*380*	*301*	*79*
French Canadian	165	108	57	48	24	24
Italian	133	125	8	78	74	4
Polish	110	90	20	67	58	9
Irish	79	60	19	14	3	11
Canadian	54	39	15	21	17	4
Russian	41	39	2	21	20	1
German	28	9	19	14	3	11
Portuguese	28	28	..	8	8	..
Lithuanian	27	24	3	13	12	1
English	26	19	7	11	7	4
Scotch	17	12	5	7	6	1
Austrian	15	10	5	8	5	3
Danish	11	8	3	..	..	..
Armenian	10	10	..	8	8	..
Swedish	9	6	3	6	4	2
Spanish	7	7	..	3	3	..
French	6	1	5	6	1	5
Russian Jew	4	4	..	4	4	..
Ukrainian	4	3	1	2	2	..
Swiss	4	4	..	3	3	..
Greek	3	3	..	1	1	..
Czecho-Slovak	2	2	..	..	..	..
Finnish	2	2	..	2	2	..
Jugo-Slav	2	2	..	2	2	..
Belgian	1	1	..	..	..	..
Danish-Russian	1	1	..	..	..	..
Norwegian	1	1	..	1	1	..
Welsh	1	1	..	..	..	..

The first point of interest is the ratio of foreign-born for each nationality. A long list of nationalities, headed by the Portuguese with 28 workers, had no native-born representatives whatever. Certain other nationalities were almost in the same class. Only 8 Italians out of 133 were native-born, and only 2 Russians out of 41, 3 Lithuanians out of 27, 20 Poles out of 110, etc. The French-Canadians, surprisingly enough, had a comparatively high proportion of native-born (about one-third) while two nationalities only (German and French) had more native-born than foreign.

The second set of columns in the table shows that the sampling problem was largely one of nationality. The small numbers do not count and may be ignored. There are a few nationalities which are distinctly under-represented in the schedules obtained. The Danes out of 11 workers had no returns, the Portuguese out of 28 had only 8 returns, and the French Canadians out of 165 had only 48. To a somewhat lesser extent, English-speaking Canadians with 21 returns out of 54, and the English with 11 out of 26, were also slightly under-represented.

The under-representation of these various nationalities was not due to any one cause. The Danes were mostly agricultural laborers who had gone back to the farm. The Portuguese had come to Hartford from Rhode Island and other eastern centers, and are known to have returned there when business conditions became poor. But the two Canadian nationalities are more distinctly immigrant in character. It seems probable that the French-Canadians are the advance guard of an army of immigrants coming down from Canada and northern New England. Apparently they have recently invaded Hartford, but only as migrant workers and not as permanent settlers.

It may be that both groups of Canadians are partially taking the place of European immigrants who formerly provided a mobile labor reserve for the industries of this country. The Europeans flocked in during the years of prosperity and returned home in large numbers when depression began. The stoppage of immigration during the War, followed by the subsequent restriction, has prevented this from happening for about two decades. The Canadians may be partly supplying this need for labor for expansion purposes; they are attracted to the United States during the period of prosperity and return home in time of depression. The example of Hartford is, however, not of sufficient size to justify any general conclusions. The extent to which Canada may be furnishing a mobile labor reserve for the industries of this country could only be determined by more detailed study.

The nationality composition of the Candee plant was quite different.

TABLE 5

Nationality Groups, Excluding Americans, Classified by Birthplace, Showing Schedules Obtained

NEW HAVEN

Nationality	Total Number of Workers			Schedules		
	Total	Foreign-born	Native-born	Total	Foreign-born	Native-born
Totals	*665*	*330*	*335*	*618*	*304*	*314*
Italian	417	193	224	398	184	214
Polish	79	44	35	69	40	29
Irish	50	19	31	46	17	29
Lithuanian	32	28	4	29	26	3
German	25	11	14	22	10	12
French-Canadian	8	5	3	7	4	3
Austrian	7	5	2	6	4	2
Russian	7	4	3	7	4	3
Scotch	6	5	1	5	4	1
Swedish	6	4	2	5	3	2
Canadian	4	2	2	3	1	2
French	4	1	3	4	1	3
Ukrainian	4	3	1	4	3	1
Slavic	4	..	4	4	..	4
English	3	1	2	3	1	2
Belgian	2	..	2	2	..	2
Danish	2	..	2	2	..	2
Greek	1	1	..	1	1	..
Norwegian	1	1	..	1	1	..
Cuban	1	1	..	..	..	..
Portuguese	1	1	..	..	..	..
Venezuelan	1	1	..	..	..	..

It is clear that this plant was completely dominated by Italians who constituted about 63 per cent of all foreign nationalities. The Canadians here were insignificant in numbers, and they were not at all migratory, as is shown by the fact that all but one of them were successfully surveyed. There was only one Portuguese. Thus the New Haven plant had very few representatives of the migratory nationalities.

While the Candee working force at the time of the shutdown was very settled and stable, a cross-classification of nationality by age groups furnishes concrete evidence of previous waves of migration to New Haven. The facts are presented in the accompanying chart.

The Irish furnish the best example of the point. Judged by the number of older workers in the plant at the time of the shut-

CHART I

LEADING NATIONALITIES IN NEW HAVEN PLANT CLASSIFIED BY AGE AND PLACE OF BIRTH

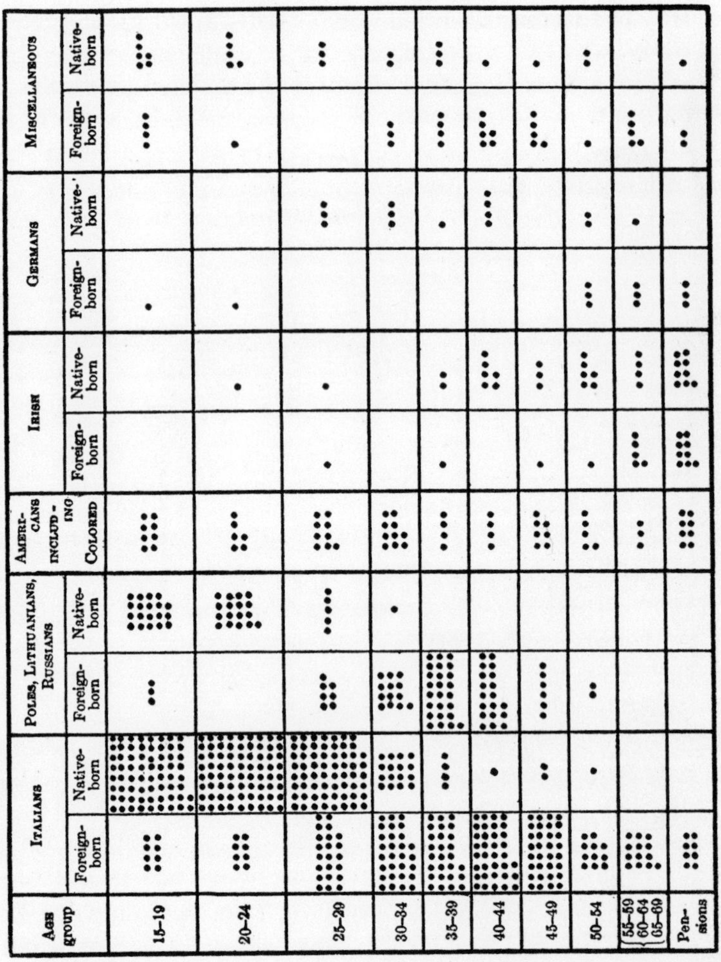

Age group	Italians Foreign-born	Italians Native-born	Poles, Lithuanians, Russians Foreign-born	Poles, Lithuanians, Russians Native-born	Americans including Colored	Irish Foreign-born	Irish Native-born	Germans Foreign-born	Germans Native-born	Miscellaneous Foreign-born	Miscellaneous Native-born
15–19											
20–24											
25–29											
30–34											
35–39											
40–44											
45–49											
50–54											
55–59 60–64 65–69											
Pen-sions											

down, the Irish must have been one of the dominant nationalities in the plant in the late decades of the last century, although, as shown by the proportion of native and foreign-born, they were not exactly a migrant group at that time. The chart shows that no fewer than 27 out of 50 were above fifty-five years of age, while only 3 lone members were under thirty-five. With the coming of the Italians and Slavs, the Irish deserted the rubber industry, or at least carefully kept their children away from it. The Germans, like the Irish, seem also to have avoided the industry. The heavy proportion of Italians and Slavs in the middle-aged classes shows that these were first-generation immigrants, who took the place of the Irish and Germans. In recent years the working force had been recruited chiefly from the second (native-born) generation of these "new" immigrant races, and, in a surprisingly large number of cases, even from the children of these older Candee workers.

Length of Service

The labor mobility thus found to be concentrated in certain nationality groups would naturally express itself in the service records of the workers. These were examined with a view to determining the relative stability of the working forces in the two plants. The next table summarizes the length of service of the New Haven workers.

Because of the variable meanings of the term "length of service," the data have been expressed in two different ways. One of these was the Company's official service record, defined as the time worked since the last break in service. The meaning of "break" was not defined with any great precision, however. Generally speaking, it meant continuous service with the Company at all times when the plant was in operation, except for certain excusable absences such as those involving illness, accident, vacation, army war service, and (in the case of women) childbirth. Six months was considered to be the maximum time allowed, although for war service and childbirth as much as two years or more was sanctioned in certain cases. However, any absence due to the worker's employment by another company was considered to constitute a break in service, regardless of the time involved.

The difficulty about this last point is that the Candee plant often closed down for extended periods. There were usually two different two-week periods of layoff every year for inventory and other purposes, and in certain depression years these normal closings were extended to about two months. Instead of remaining idle the workers would usually scout around for another job, which they would hold until the rubber company sent a call announcing the re-opening of the factory. Practically all the workers immediately flocked back to work, partly because they considered that their regular job and partly because they much preferred to work there. But occasionally a worker would stay on where he was for some weeks or months before returning (some, of course, never came back). In such case the Company, under its official definition, considered him to have broken his service record, while the worker often felt his conduct fully justified. Up until the time of the final shutdown this point remained purely an academic one for all except those employes who were working toward their pensions. But when the dismissal wage payments were based upon length of service, some workers found themselves ineligible under the strict official rule. There were no bitter disputes about the matter, but some workers felt that they had suffered unduly from a rather formal ruling. Under the circumstances the Company was most lenient in interpreting all border-line cases, but this did not solve the problem entirely.

TABLE 6

Average Length of Service by Age
Surveyed Workers Only

NEW HAVEN

AGE GROUPS	Official Length of Service (years)	Total Working Time (years)
All Workers	*8.4*	*9.9*
15–19	1.4	1.5
20–24	4.2	4.8
25–29	5.9	7.9
30–34	4.8	6.9
35–39	6.2	8.3
40–44	8.2	9.8
45 and over	14.7	17.4
Pensioners	34.3	34.8

Apart from these cases, there were many workers, especially among the women, who had worked in the plant prior to marriage, dropped out after marriage, and then returned years later. Many of them had never worked for any other concern, and in more ways than one their total working time represented their true service record. In order to present an adequate picture of the length of service of these New Haven workers, the averages for both the official service and the total working time are shown for each age group. Total working time is defined as the total time worked for the Company since the first date of hiring, deductions being made for time actually lost, but not for breaks in service.

The spread between the official length of service and the total working time is evident in all age groups. For the entire factory it amounted to 1.5 years in a total of 9.9. As between age groups it is of interest to note that the workers 25–29 years old had a better average service record than the next older group 30–34. The long service of those over 45 is clearly shown, and the pensioners established the remarkable record of nearly 35 years of service on the average.

TABLE 7

Length of Service
Surveyed Workers Only
New Haven

LENGTH OF SERVICE (Years)	NUMBER OF WORKERS	
	Official Length of Service	Total Working Time
Totals.....................................	*672*	*672*
Less than year..........................	97	71
1–2..	99	66
2–3..	51	83
3–4..	55	52
4–5..	22	18
5–6..	41	35
6–7..	30	43
7–8..	19	26
8–9..	25	38
9–10..	24	35
10–11.......................................	39	48
11–12.......................................	27	36
12–13.......................................	19	19
13–14.......................................	14	18
14–15.......................................	3	6
15–19.......................................	28	34
20–24.......................................	14	20
25–29.......................................	13	14
30–34.......................................	12	16
35–39.......................................	20	22
40–44.......................................	10	12
45 and over...............................	3	3
No Report..................................	7	7

Since the averages conceal the variations between the individual workers, the data are presented in another form, showing the classification of workers according to length of service regardless of age.

On the basis of official length of service 196 workers, or nearly 30 per cent of the total number, had been with the Company less than two years. On total working time, about 20 per cent of the workers had joined the force within two years of March, 1929. A classification by age groups shows that the vast majority of these were young people, considerably more than half being under twenty. Yet these young people were found and surveyed, a fact which indicates that they were permanent residents of the city. There was no difficulty about the surveyed group not being representative of the entire force with respect to length of service.

The long records of service at the New Haven plant are clearly shown in total working time. About 37 per cent of the force had worked 10 years or more; 121 individuals had exceeded 15 years, and 87 had records of 20 years and over. The figures give evidence of the stability and loyalty of the working force.

A sharply contrasting situation existed in the Hartford plant, where the average length of service, on a total working time basis, was only 5.4 years, as compared with 9.9 in New Haven. There were only a handful of extra-long-service workers in Hartford, and a very large proportion of men in the groups under two years.

The bearing of this situation upon the survey will be apparent from the following table showing length of service on the basis of total working time only.

Note in the first column the marked difference in the distribution as compared with the similar distribution for New Haven (Table 7). Proportionately the number in the first two groups was very much greater in Hartford, and the number in all groups over 15 years was considerably less.

Contrary also to New Haven experience is the fact that short service is not closely correlated with age. The number of workers in the Hartford plant under 20 years of age was negligible; there were many short-service men in all groups up to 35 years of age, and there was even a sprinkling of them in the 40's. In other words many older workers had only recently joined the force.

The last two columns show the varying proportions of schedules obtained in the field for each service group. Note the low coverage among the short-service men, and the correspondingly

TABLE 8

Length of Service (Total Working Time)
Showing Sample Obtained
Total Force
HARTFORD

LENGTH OF SERVICE (Years)	Total Number of Workers	NUMBER OF WORKERS	
		Scheduled	Not Found
Totals............................	*1105*	*534*	*571*
Less than year....................	221	71	150
1–2...............................	215	79	186
2–3...............................	67	38	29
3–4...............................	58	20	38
4–5...............................	84	39	45
5–6...............................	43	24	19
6–7...............................	95	55	40
7–8...............................	31	15	16
8–9...............................	31	15	16
9–10..............................	39	26	13
10–11.............................	52	36	16
11–12.............................	31	20	11
12–13.............................	20	12	8
13–14.............................	20	14	6
14–15.............................	21	13	8
15–19.............................	53	39	14
20–24.............................	12	9	3
25–29.............................	8	7	1
30–34.............................	3	1	2
35–39.............................	1	1	..

higher coverage among the long-service workers. Only about one-third of those under two years' service were found, while the ratio for men of 9 years and upward was more than two-thirds.

Even this analysis does not touch the heart of the problem. There was clearly present in Hartford some factor which was absent in New Haven—a factor which could probably not have been isolated had it not been for the fact that the survey in two cities made it possible to use one as a control on the other. This factor expressed itself (as shown by the Hartford sample obtained in the field work) through age, nationality, and service record, although these in themselves were wholly superficial. The younger workers were somewhat harder to locate for survey purposes, but age was not the crucial point, as the New Haven results show. Canadians and Portuguese were obviously a footloose group of workers, but it was not their nationality that made them so; these workers are not by nature any more unstable than others. Short-service workers were difficult to find in Hartford, but they gave no trouble at all in New Haven. The conclusion must be that the short-service workers in Hartford, who were mostly Canadians and Portuguese, constituted a migratory character which prevented them from being represented in the sample obtained.

Thus we are brought at last to the final point: namely, that the basic factor in this whole problem was an economic one— the condition of business. In this respect the two cities differed radically. For some years New Haven had not been expanding very rapidly in an industrial way, nor had existing industries as a whole enjoyed any high degree of prosperity. Following the war-time boom some of the city's leading firms found themselves in a greatly over-expanded condition, from which recovery had been rather slow. The curve of industrial employment had shown no appreciable upward trend for some years prior to 1929, and there was little incentive for migrant industrial workers to stop in the city. Much of the growth that did take place was in various "sweated" trades employing women almost exclusively.

Hartford, on the contrary, had been industrially prosperous for many years, and the last boom (1928–29) brought about a significant increase in the city's industrial wage-earning population. Hence the city furnished an attractive labor market, especially to men drifting away from the depressed textile centers of northern and eastern New England.

It was these migratory workers who were missed in the survey. The results obtained and the conclusions drawn are valid only for the more stable workers, the permanent residents. In New Haven this meant practically the entire working force so that the findings for that city apply to the plant as a whole. In Hartford, however, the sample is adequate and representative for permanent residents only; the findings do not apply to migratory workers.

In one sense this makes the final results in New Haven and Hartford more directly comparable. Similar groups of workers were covered in the two places. It is necessary only to keep in mind, in interpreting the data presented in the next chapter, that a certain section of the working force in the Hartford plant were not covered at all, and that therefore the conclusions do not apply to them as such.

II. THE INDUSTRIAL READJUSTMENT OF THE WORKERS

For practically all the workers involved in the shutdown, except those placed on a pension and a few who were transferred to other plants of the Company, the pressing and immediate problem was that of finding another job. It is important, then, to see just what success attended the efforts of these workers, aided by the company, the city government, industrial organizations, and miscellaneous agencies.

LENGTH OF TIME OUT OF WORK

There were a few workers who were reported as not having looked for work during the period from the shutdown to the date of interview. Out of 534 workers surveyed in Hartford only 9 were so recorded, while among the 672 in New Haven, no less than 84 did not try to find work. The sharp contrast between the two cities can be largely attributed to the sex differences in the working forces. In New Haven the women comprised the bulk of those not seeking work—69 women as compared to 15 men. These were for the most part housewives or older women who decided to retire from industry.

The above workers had to be carefully distinguished from those who did not succeed in finding work, of whom there were 83 in Hartford and 68 in New Haven. It was sometimes difficult to decide in which of these two groups a worker should be classified. For those who admitted not having looked for work, the worker's own statement was taken at its face value. But if a worker claimed he could not find work, efforts were made by the interviewer to discover how seriously he had tried. Older men beyond the age of retirement, and housewives who might have been inclined to quit work anyhow, were questioned closely as to their job-hunting activities. In all cases of doubt the decision was made against the worker, that is, everyone who could possibly be classed as not having looked for work was put in that group. This was done in order that the group listed as not being

21

able to find a job in nearly a year of effort should not be exaggerated in the figures on length of time out of work.

A summary view of the duration of unemployment is shown in Table 9:[1]

TABLE 9

Length of Time Necessary to Find Work
Total number of workers seeking work and number finding first permanent job within a period of approximately two months, classified by age groups*

| AGE GROUPS | HARTFORD | | NEW HAVEN | | | |
| | | | MEN | | WOMEN | |
	Total Number Seeking Work	Number Finding First Job in 0, 1, or 2 Months	Total Number Seeking Work	Number Finding First Job in 0, 1, or 2 Months	Total Number Seeking Work	Number Finding First Job in 0, 1, or 2 Months
Total	*523*	*305*	*228*	*140*	*358*	*231*
15–19	9	5	23	17	77	58
20–24	45	25	18	10	75	54
25–29	80	53	26	17	72	47
30–34	90	56	28	19	33	24
35–39	108	62	23	15	35	14
40–44	88	50	32	29	30	18
45–49	50	28	30	15	17	8
50–54	26	14	19	11	10	5
55–59	13	9	15	4	1	1
60–64	8	3	6	2	1	0
65–69	3	0	1	1	0	0
Pensions	3	0	7	0	7	2

* In classifying the time out of work, 0 means two weeks or less, 1 means from half a month to a month and a half, 2 months equals from one and one-half to two and one-half months, etc. This method of tabulation was used because of the tendency of the workers to reply in round numbers; it is a more satisfactory classification than the method of breaking the class groups at exactly one month, two months, etc. The complete table on time out of work is shown in the appendix.

This shows the relationships existing between the total number who tried to find work and the number who found it in a period of 0, 1, or 2 months—that is, how many found work in a period of somewhat less than three months.

In this tabulation strictly temporary jobs were not counted. Such jobs, while they might help the worker tide himself and his family over the unemployment period, do not represent a permanent adjustment—he must keep on the lookout for another job.

[1] For complete details by months, see Tables 35H and 35N in the Appendix D. For comparative data from other studies, see Myers, R. J., *Occupational Readjustment of Displaced Skilled Workmen*, Jour. Pol. Econ., August, 1929; and Lubin, Isador, *The Absorption of the Unemployed by American Industry*, Brookings Institution, Pamphlet Series Vol. I, No. 3, Washington, D. C., 1929.

However, it was not in principle but in practice that the chief difficulties in classifying jobs occurred. Some few jobs were amenable to simple objective tests—picking up paper in the city parks during July and August, or helping in the postoffice during the Christmas holidays, would be considered temporary, for there is a definite end in sight in each case. But the status of most jobs had to be determined by a purely subjective test— the worker's impression of the situation. A man who took a job as substitute truck driver during the regular driver's illness could have been under no illusion as to the temporary character of the work. On the other hand, a mechanic who took a job as drill press operator in a machine shop with the understanding that he was to be the regular man must be credited with a permanent job, even though he was laid off a month later because of slack times. In this latter case the job was offered and accepted in good faith on a permanent basis; unforeseen events later altered the situation. In other words, the prospects of the job at the time of acceptance, rather than the length of time held or the eventual outcome, constitute an arbitrary but convenient test of permanence.

On the whole there was little difference between the two sexes in respect to the time it took to find the first job; sex seems to be a negligible factor, but it is very clear that age is not. The marked success of the younger workers is shown for both sexes, while the handicap to workers over forty-five is equally apparent. Of all men over forty-five actively seeking work, only 43 per cent found jobs in the specified time, while of those under forty-five over 71 per cent were in this class. For the women the corresponding percentages are 44 and 67. The contrast between young and old is further sharpened if those who never succeeded in finding work during the survey period are taken into consideration. Of the 28 men of all ages who failed in their quest no less than 22 were over forty-five years old.

In Hartford, variations with respect to age were quite different from those in New Haven. There was much greater uniformity among all age groups, and the sharp differentiation between youth and age was not in evidence. The best record was made by workers of 25–34 years, while the young men fell below the average. There is a noticeable downward tendency in the percentages of the older groups which cannot be obscured by the rather freakish performance of the group 55–59.

The two "sport" groups in New Haven—men 40–44 and women 35–39—deserve attention. These men made the best record of any group, while the women of practically the same age had the worst luck of all. The factor concealed in this situation is that of occupation: the men held jobs which were similar to those in many other industries; the women were the old handicraft shoemakers, whose occupation disappeared with the new improved processes.[1]

Analysis of the data shows clearly that there was very little difference between Hartford and New Haven in the duration of unemployment. This is surprising in view of the much more aggressive and well-organized efforts made in Hartford by industry and the community.

These efforts, strange to say, seem to have had little statistically observable effect. One explanation of this can be found in the state of business. Both shutdowns were timed to catch the seasonal expansion in trade, one in the Spring, the other in the Fall. The seasonal expansion in New Haven was largely counterbalanced by the slow cyclical decline of business which had already set in and which continued gently through the Summer. The Hartford shutdown, however, ran squarely into a sweeping decline which quickly achieved the proportions of a major depression. It is probable that, without the powerful community coöperation instituted in Hartford, the unemployment experiences of the workers would have been much worse. At the same time, the cold facts embodied in the statistics cannot fail to furnish some evidence of the helplessness of good wishes in the face of economic forces. Emergency programs,

---

[1] E. D. Smith makes the point that the problem of the middle-aged worker in industry is not a matter of age but of obsolescence. He cites examples of even comparatively young workers whose training and experience have been so narrow that they have become inflexible and unadaptable. See Smith, E. D., *What are the Psychological Factors of Obsolescence of Workers in Middle Age?* Personnel Series No. 9. American Management Association, New York, 1930.

The skilled shoemakers mentioned in the text above had had very narrow, specialized training and they were probably the least adaptable group laid off in the shutdown. The extremely poor results achieved by these workers in finding satisfactory new jobs is ample demonstration of the point.

community goodwill, and all the other forms of coöperation did not, in this case at least, seriously modify the usual course of events.

LENGTH OF TIME ON FIRST PERMANENT JOB

A somewhat different view of the problem of reabsorption is obtained from the data on the length of time the first permanent job was held. Did the worker like the job so well, and was he so satisfactory to the employer that he was still employed at it when the survey was made? Or was there a severance of relations between employer and employe very soon after the hiring? The chief point of interest here is the number of workers who held their first job straight through. This is shown in the summary table below.

TABLE 10

Length of Time on First Permanent Job

Total number of workers finding work at any time and number holding first permanent job through to the closing date of the survey, classified by age groups

	HARTFORD		NEW HAVEN			
			MEN		WOMEN	
AGE GROUPS	Total Number Finding Work at Any Time	Number Holding First Job through to Closing Date	Total Number Finding Work at Any Time	Number Holding First Job through to Closing Date	Total Number Finding Work at Any Time	Number Holding First Job through to Closing Date
Total	*441*	*253*	*201*	*100*	*319*	*140*
15–19	7	2	22	7	72	29
20–24	39	20	18	5	72	23
25–29	70	46	23	13	63	35
30–34	81	41	28	13	30	13
35–39	93	54	21	11	36	12
40–44	77	46	32	17	25	10
45–49	42	20	26	15	16	9
50–54	22	13	13	6	9	5
55–59	10	6	9	6	1	0
60–64	3	2	4	3	1	1
65–69	2	2	1	0	0	0
Pensions	1	1	4	4	4	3

The permanence of the new job in Hartford turned out to be somewhat greater than in New Haven. In the former the number of men holding their first job straight through to the closing date of the survey constituted over 57 per cent of those finding work at any time in the interval, while in New Haven the corresponding percentage was 46. In view of the fact that the Hart-

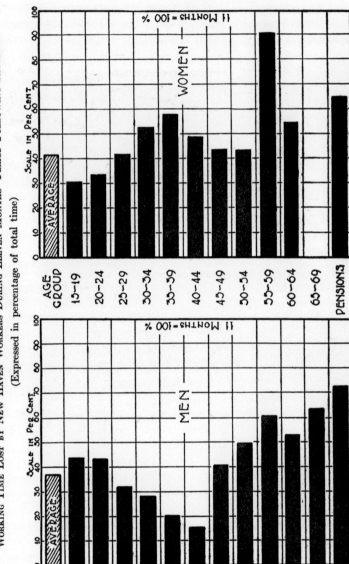

CHART II

WORKING TIME LOST BY NEW HAVEN WORKERS DURING ELEVEN MONTHS' PERIOD FOLLOWING SHUTDOWN

(Expressed in percentage of total time)

ford sample contains only the more permanent residents of the city (the newcomers having left), the two groups should be about on a par in general stability of residence and attitude. The chief difference lies in the class of workmen involved. The greater skill, better earning capacity, and higher social level of the men in the Hartford plant probably account for the fact that they were better able to get new jobs satisfactory to themselves, and also that they proved to be more desirable workmen. In addition, this may have been one way in which community effort was effective. The high degree of industrial coöperation and goodwill attained there undoubtedly led to the opening up of high-grade jobs in the very best plants in the city where stability was an important feature.

With respect to this point, sex differences seem again unimportant, although in the two younger groups the women make a slightly better showing than the men. With reference to age, however, those under twenty-five years have considerably lower stability than the older workers of both sexes. Of the women finding work at all, 44 per cent held their jobs right through to the end, but the percentage for the two youngest age groups was about 36 as compared to about 50 for the remainder. It is scarcely conceivable that the latter were more adaptable to change, nor is it likely that the greater time required to find work resulted in any better choice of jobs. We shall probably be closer to the facts if we assume that the older workers, appreciating fully their more precarious position in the industrial world, clung to their jobs with more tenacity.

TOTAL WORKING TIME LOST

A third type of summary is developed in the analysis of the total time out of work throughout the survey period, computed as a weighted average. For this summary, allowance is made for all temporary jobs, since the object is to determine the actual amount of lost time.

On the whole there was comparatively little difference between the two places. For the entire working force in New Haven the average time lost was 4.38 months, or approximately 40 per cent of the available time over a period of 11 months.

CHART III

Working Time Lost by Hartford Workers During Ten Months' Period Following Shutdown

(Expressed in percentage of full time)

Scale in Per Cent

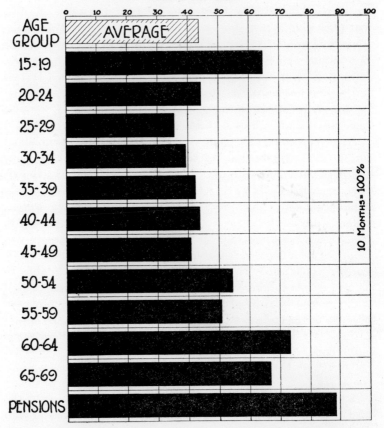

The average time lost by the Hartford workers was 4.33 months in a total of 10, or about 43 per cent of available time—certainly not far out of line with New Haven results.[1]

Despite the greater tenacity displayed by the older workers, age still appears to be a handicap, regardless of sex. On the

[1] Myers (op. cit., p. 479) reports an average loss of time amounting to 5.2 months, but the data are not quite comparable to those given here.

other hand, youth reacted quite differently in the two sexes, for the two youngest women's groups established the low record of 3.5 months of lost time, while the young men of the same age averaged about 4.8 months, a figure surpassed only by men over fifty. Still further, the middle-aged men lost the least time, those 35–44 losing less than 2.0 months, although women of the corresponding ages were establishing poor records. These variations with respect to sex grow partly out of the occupational differences previously cited, and partly out of the industrial structure of New Haven, which is heavily weighted with industries employing women.

The concentration of heavy losses of time in the very old and the very young (so characteristic of the men in New Haven) appears again in much milder form in Hartford.

The low record for lost time was established by men age 25–34, although the variation from the over-all average was much less pronounced than in New Haven. Workers over fifty and those under twenty all lost more than half of the possible working time.

EMPLOYMENT AT END OF PERIOD

The last analysis of the relationship of jobs and time involves merely the count of those workers who were actually holding a permanent job at the time the survey ended. Knowing that, say, on April 1, 1929, *all* New Haven workers were employed, we can sum up the net result of the shutdown and the readjustment by finding out how many were employed on March 1, 1930; or, for Hartford, September 1 and July 1, respectively. The results for both cities are shown in the table below.

In absolute terms approximately 70 per cent of the men, and 77 per cent of the women in New Haven were actually working in some job at the end of eleven months. The distribution by age groups is again significant, and it will be noticed that the two youngest men's groups are again out of line here, averaging only 56 per cent at work as compared to 70 per cent for all men.

The similarity between the two plants is quite marked. In both New Haven and Hartford practically 70 per cent of the men workers were employed at the close of the study. This

TABLE 11

Workers Employed at Closing Date of Survey

Number of workers actively seeking work during survey period and holding jobs at closing date, classified by age groups.

AGE GROUPS	HARTFORD		NEW HAVEN			
			MEN		WOMEN	
	Total Number Actively Seeking Work	Number of Workers Employed July 1, 1930	Total Number Actively Seeking Work	Number of Workers Employed March 1, 1930	Total Number Actively Seeking Work	Number of Workers Employed March 1, 1930
Total	*523*	*364*	*227*	*158*	*323*	*247*
15–19	9	3	23	13	71	58
20–24	45	30	18	10	67	56
25–29	79	64	26	21	63	51
30–34	91	64	27	23	27	19
35–39	109	81	23	19	33	22
40–44	88	57	32	29	27	19
45–49	50	35	31	21	17	12
50–54	26	18	19	9	10	6
55–59	12	7	14	6	0	0
60–64	8	2	6	3	1	1
65–69	3	2	1	0	0	0
Pensions	3	1	7	4	7	3

represents a somewhat more favorable showing for New Haven, considering the larger proportion of older men in that factory. The best age group in Hartford was 25–29 with a record of 81 per cent employment, as against 74 per cent for those 35–39. There was the same shading off toward the extremes—both the old men and young men fared worse than the middle-aged.

QUALITY OF NEW JOBS OBTAINED

In analyzing the time element in the unemployment situation we ignored for the moment another dimension of the problem. To appraise the true condition of the unemployed worker we need to know not merely the amount of time lost, but also the quality of the jobs held when work was found. Many factors could conceivably enter into this analysis of quality, but study of this particular situation indicated that psychic and other factors were heavily weighted in favor of the old job with the rubber company; therefore, to make the comparison conservative, these intangibles have been entirely eliminated, and the measurement of quality has been based upon the objective and significant test of *wage rates*. The question has been put in this form: How many workers obtained any *permanent* new job paying wages

(weekly) at least as high as those paid by the United States
Rubber Company?

The answers to this question give a still clearer impression of
the setback experienced by the workers in the shutdowns.
Thus, only 61 men in New Haven were able to get a job paying
as well as the old one, while 130 men failed in this respect. For
the women the corresponding figures were 76 and 235, a considerably lower proportion than in the case of the men. Women
of practically all ages fared worse than the men in their new
jobs.[1]

TABLE 12

Changes in Wage Rates

Number of workers finding work and obtaining any new job paying as high wages
as the old one, classified by age groups

	HARTFORD		NEW HAVEN			
			MEN		WOMEN	
AGE GROUPS	Total Number Finding Work	Number Obtaining Any New Job Paying as High Wages as Old Job	Total Number Finding Work	Number Obtaining Any New Job Paying as High Wages as Old Job	Total Number Finding Work	Number Obtaining Any New Job Paying as High Wages as Old Job
Total	*420*	*37*	*191*	*61*	*311*	*76*
15–19	7	2	22	12	72	32
20–24	35	2	18	9	69	12
25–29	68	5	23	7	59	9
30–34	81	12	27	8	30	10
35–39	88	10	18	3	26	2
40–44	64	3	29	8	25	3
45–49	41	3	24	7	16	4
50–54	20	0	13	3	8	2
55–59	10	0	9	1	1	1
60–64	3	0	3	1	1	1
65–69	2	0	1	0	0	0
Pensions	1	0	4	2	4	0

Age proves not to be particularly significant on this point,
except for the extreme youngsters. The difference (for both

[1] Lubin (op. cit., p. 12) reported 46 per cent of the workers earning as much on
the new jobs as on the old. Eliminating the cases on which he obtained no information, his men are split almost half and half on the question of earnings.

Myers (op. cit., p. 485) found about 54 per cent of the cutters in jobs paying
wages at least equal to the rates on the old jobs.

It is very probable that the business depression partially accounts for this difference, although this has been allowed for to some extent by the use of full-time earnings in preference to actual earnings on the new job. Even this procedure, however,
cannot provide an allowance for the lack of new opportunities available and for the
rather unsatisfactory jobs which often had to be accepted by the workers.

sexes) between those under twenty years of age and the rest of the force is very striking. In other words, it was the young apprentices and beginners who bettered themselves. When the gains and losses given in Table 6 were further analyzed to show the number of those getting (or suffering) various percentages of gain (or loss) the results were even more significant.

The gains turned out to be slight, while the losses were heavy. One-third of those reporting a new job paying as well as the old merely succeeded in equaling their former wage rates. The median increase for women fell between 10 and 20 per cent, while for men it was less than 10 per cent. On the other hand, the decreases in wages were not only two times (men) and three times (women) as numerous as the gains, but they were also far more severe. The median losses in wage rates, both for men and women, fell in the class from 30 to 40 per cent, and losses running up to 50 and 60 per cent were not uncommon. Whatever may be thought about the wage scales paid at the rubber company plant, they must be rated as very good in comparison with the wages received by the workers on subsequent jobs. Furthermore, these comparisons are for the *best* job ever held in the interval, and *no account whatever is taken of workers who found no jobs at all.*

Hartford results were even worse. Scarcely 9 per cent of the men were able to report any new job paying as well as the old, and half of these got no better than an even break, leaving a mere handful fortunate enough to come out ahead. In Hartford, too, the median decrease was in the class 30 to 40 per cent.

The best method of synthesizing these results is to combine both gains and losses in a general table of average wages. A multitude of interesting points can be found in this table, but only a few can be mentioned here. For one thing, the wage rates of the men averaged approximately 50 per cent higher than those of the women, both in the old jobs and in the new. Secondly, both sexes suffered heavy losses in earning capacity, the men's wages slightly exceeding 80 per cent of the old rates, while the women barely attained 76 per cent. Generally speaking, throughout all age groups, the women came off second-best to the men in the new jobs. Thirdly, youth made out much better than age. For the men there is almost a steady decline in the relative percentages from youth to age; men under twenty were the only age group to make a real gain in wages. The same tendencies are observable, though less clearly defined, in the women's percentages. Fourthly, the occupational status of certain workers, previously noted, comes to light in these figures. The women, 35–39, who as shoemakers made the highest wages in the plant among their sex, made the poorest readjustment and came out with practically the lowest wages. Likewise, the good records made by those under twenty of both sexes can be partly attributed to their beginning or apprenticeship status with its consequent low wages.

TABLE 13

Comparison of Wage Rates, New Haven

Average weekly earnings before and after shutdown, by sex and age groups

	MEN			WOMEN		
AGE GROUPS	Number Reporting Comparable Wage Rates	Average Weekly Earnings		Number Reporting Comparable Wage Rates	Average Weekly Earnings	
		Rubber Company 1928	Best-Paid Job 1929–30		Rubber Company 1928	Best-Paid Job 1929–30
Total	*187*	*31.42*	*25.26*	*306*	*20.65*	*15.68*
15–19	22	17.82	19.27	72	17.44	15.95
20–24	18	27.08	24.97	69	21.34	16.05
25–29	21	34.64	29.40	59	22.08	15.83
30–34	27	34.24	27.17	29	21.26	17.33
35–39	18	33.92	25.97	25	23.94	13.88
40–44	29	33.78	27.05	23	22.32	15.70
45–49	23	32.86	25.47	16	20.38	13.38
50–54	13	33.58	24.50	8	17.31	14.19
55–59	9	36.78	22.89	1	10.50	14.00
60–64	3	29.33	24.67	0	....	....
Pensions	4	28.50	15.63	4	21.00	14.13

In the Hartford data the most significant facts are: (1) the greater decline in wage rates as compared with New Haven, and (2) the marked similarity of this decline in practically all age groups; a very slight downward trend from youth to age can be discerned, but it is unimportant. The severe decline in wages among the Hartford workers—to 70 per cent as against 80 per cent for men in New Haven—is not due to the poor quality of the new jobs (which will be seen to average higher in absolute wage rates than did those in New Haven) but to the higher wage level existing in the Hartford factory. All the middle-aged groups there were averaging $38–39 per week, and even the youngest, lowest-paid group was just under $29. In other words, the fall was greater because the peak had been higher.

ANNUAL INCOME

The final estimate of the displaced worker's change in well-being depends not alone upon time lost or wage rates obtained, but upon the combination of these two, i. e., upon income received. In view of the more nearly complete coverage of the entire working force obtained in the New Haven survey, and also of the better quality of data collected there, a special computation on annual income has been made for the workers in

TABLE 14

Comparison of Wage Rates, Hartford

Average weekly earnings before and after shutdown, by age groups

AGE GROUPS	Number Reporting Comparable Wage Rates	AVERAGE WEEKLY EARNINGS	
		Rubber Company Jan.-Aug. 1929	Best-paid Job 1929–30
Total	*405*	*37.15*	*26.16*
15–19...........................	7	28.71	22.14
20–24...........................	33	32.80	24.24
25–29...........................	68	35.52	25.16
30–34...........................	81	37.72	26.99
35–39...........................	81	38.41	26.95
40–44...........................	62	39.35	26.90
45–49...........................	40	38.88	28.14
50–54...........................	19	36.55	22.87
55–59...........................	9	32.61	23.00
60–64...........................	3	38.17	27.00
65–69...........................	1	34.00	25.00
Pensions.....................	1	49.50	15.00

that plant. Such a comparison should put the finishing touches on the appraisal of the shutdown's effects.

The total annual earnings of the individual workers at the rubber shop were collected from the 1928 income tax cards. This was the last full year the plant operated prior to the shutdown, and it was a normal year in most respects. Against these figures for each individual worker has been set up the estimated total earnings for the period April 1, 1929, to April 1, 1930—one full year following the shutdown. The estimates have been based upon the length of time worked on each job and the corresponding wage rates reported for each worker. Space forbids a complete discussion of the detailed methods used in making such estimates. No attempt has been made to use the data for each individual in any way, but, combined by age and sex groups, the group totals have been directly compared: 1928 earnings with the rubber company versus 1929–30 earnings for one year following the shutdown. Those who actively sought work (even though they never found it) have been included with zero or temporary-job earnings for the second year; those not looking for a job have been excluded, as have pensioners and certain other incomparables.

The data speak for themselves, but of course too much cannot be claimed for them. They do show that in New Haven in 1929–30 a particular group of displaced workers suffered net losses in annual earnings of approximately 50 per cent. What this means to the workers in reduced standards of living and to the business community in loss of purchasing power can better be imagined than expressed. In case raw figures seem to express it more effectively than percentages, an additional fact can be added: *for those workers included in the comparison* the total 1928 earnings slightly exceeded $500,000; the post-shutdown earnings of the same group were about $264,000.

A brief comment on the sex factor is necessary. The women's over-all average is thoroughly representative both because all age groups fared very much alike, and also because women over fifty were not numerous. The men's average, however, is unduly depressed by the disastrous decline in the earnings of the older men. If a mild allowance is made for the disproportionate weight of the older groups, it is safe to say that the men would average well above 55 per cent.

Acknowledging the possibility of a considerable margin of error in practically all the foregoing figures, and making a rough summary only, we can say in conclusion that in New Haven the typical male worker in the course of one year immediately following the shutdown suffered a loss of 37 per cent in working time, an additional loss of 20 per cent in wage rates, making a total decline of about 45 per cent in annual earnings; the typical female worker lost 40 per cent of working time, 24 per cent in wage rates, making a total loss of about 50 per cent in annual earnings.

CHART IV

ANNUAL EARNINGS OF NEW HAVEN WORKERS, 1929–30

(Expressed in percentage of 1928 annual earnings)

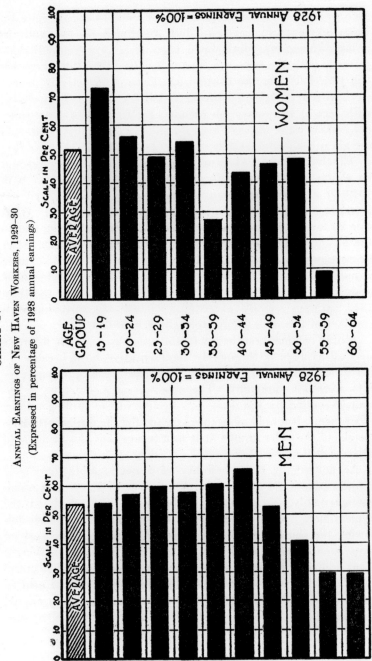

THE DISMISSAL WAGE

Of the 729 Candee workers included in this survey, 97 received a dismissal wage, the payments ranging from a minimum of $137 to a maximum of $2,088; the median payment was $402 and the average $514. Since the wage paid was equal to one week's pay for each year of service, the amount depended both upon current earnings and upon the length of time worked for the company.

The interest in these dismissal wage payments lies not so much in the purposes or philosophy of the company in paying them as in their results so far as the workers are concerned. Did these payments facilitate the readjustment of the workers, or were they in effect a mere form of relief which did little more than postpone the eventual disaster?

No less than 90 of the 97 workers (excluding foremen) receiving a dismissal wage in New Haven were found and interviewed in the course of the survey. For the most part these workers were amicably disposed toward the company and the investigators and talked very freely of their problems.

TABLE 15

Length of Time to First Permanent Job

Workers 45 years of age and over, classified into (1) those receiving a dismissal wage, and (2) those not receiving a dismissal wage

Dismissal Wage Status	Total	No. of Months to First Permanent Job												Did not Find	Did not Look
		0	1	2	3	4	5	6	7	8	9	10	Unknown		
Total	117	19	19	9	10	2	6	4	2	4	3	1	1	21	16
Dismissal Wage	73	10	13	4	7	2	6	2	1	2	2	1	..	14	9
Others	44	9	6	5	3	.	.	..	2	1	2	1	..	1	7	7

In the first place, contrary perhaps to popular expectation, they proved just as aggressive in looking for work as did any of their fellows. Some of them stated that they were using the wage as a means of retiring from active work (this was true of a few of the women), but these were very old workers who would have retired soon in any case. The others went out to look for work the day the plant was closed and were quite successful in locating jobs. The following table shows the length of time required to find work of two comparable groups of workers of the same age grouping: (1) Those receiving, and (2) those not receiving a dismissal wage. It is apparent that, month by month, the dismissal wage workers were finding jobs about as quickly as the others. There is no ground whatever for thinking that the dismissal wage operated in any way as a drag on the workers' initiative.

A second point worth noting is that those who used the dismissal wage payment to go into business for themselves were generally unsuccessful. There were less than a dozen who tried any sort of independent venture. But of those who did so the great majority failed—if not technically, at least for all practical purposes. A few cases will serve as illustrations of this point.

One man, 47 years of age, with a wife and five children to support, used his $270 dismissal wage to open up a little grocery store. He was an Italian who had worked for the company with somewhat broken service since 1918. He had no success whatever. His complaint was that when he ran on credit nobody paid, but when he demanded cash nobody bought. With such meagre capital it is not surprising that before the Winter was over he was brought to the verge of bankruptcy. His case was quite typical of those men who, after a lifetime of working for wages, attempt to change over to a business run for profit. They are usually unable to adjust themselves to the new situation.

Another striking case was that of an Italian who had established an unbroken service record of 37 years. He began work for the company at the age of 15 and at the age of 52 was earning nearly $40 a week. He received a termination wage of more than $1400. In some way one of his wife's relatives, who lived in Texas, persuaded him to move to that part of the country. He invested a large part of his wage in the purchase of a truck with which he moved himself and his family to Texas. Upon his arrival he found conditions far different from what he had expected. His money was soon used up, and in some way he lost his truck to the scheming relative. At the time the survey was made his sister in New Haven reported that the family was practically destitute and trying in every way possible to get transportation back to New Haven.

The two outstanding exceptions are worth commenting upon. One was a 64-year old Italian who had had 16 years' service in the plant. He had been a shoemaker by trade in his early life and was in fact working as a shoemaker in the plant. His dismissal wage was not exceptionally large (somewhat less than $400) but he risked it all in the establishment of a shoe repair shop. He had sufficient business insight to set up his shop in a fashionable neighborhood far from his own home. Thus he did not make the mistake which so many did of expecting to make business profits by selling to his friends and fellow workers. He charged good prices for his work and got plenty of trade. He reported that he was making considerably more money than he had ever earned at the plant. This was a most fortunate thing for him since his age would have made it practically impossible to get another factory job.

One of the women workers, 50 years of age at the time of the shutdown, had just completed a record of 12½ years' continuous service. She was not an exceptional worker, her wages at the plant averaging about $22.50 per week. Her dismissal wage amounted to about $260, on the strength of which she rented a rather large rooming house capable of housing 16 roomers. She managed the entire enterprise herself. Her husband was dead, but she had two grown children, both of whom were employed. At the time of the survey the rooming house was far from full, but the income was more than sufficient to cover the rent and other expenses of carrying the house. Most of her dismissal wage money had by this time been spent but the surplus returns from the rooming house were ample to have taken care of her even without the income from her children.

Most of the workers found it necessary to use their money for current living expenses. Nearly all of them experienced a certain amount of unemployment, and nearly all, too, suffered considerable loss in earning power on their new jobs. Consequently many of them had to draw upon the dismissal wage fund to supplement the family income. One native-born American woman went to work for the company in 1898, when she was 16 years old. At the time of the shutdown she had completed 31 years' unbroken service. She was trained as an individual shoemaker

and had considerable difficulty with the system of group work
adopted in the factory in 1926. This woman at 47 years of age
was faced with the necessity of supporting a semi-invalid sister.
Her dismissal wage of approximately $600 was used up bit by
bit, first, to tide herself and her sister over the unemployment
period, and later to supplement her meagre earnings as a maid
in a hotel. This was the job she was holding at the time of the
survey.

Examples could be multiplied many times over but they are
not necessary to prove the point. One other case is mentioned
briefly because it was such a striking one. This was the case of
a Swede, now 58 years of age, who came to this country as a
young man and obtained his first job with the company in 1889;
at the time of the closing he was a skilled cutter averaging about
$40 a week. When his first son became of working age the
father obtained for him a job at the plant, little thinking that
this would later mean that both would lose their jobs on the
same day. The boy was a skilled carpenter earning good wages
at the time of the shutdown. A second son had been permanently bedridden for six years, requiring constant medical attention. Therefore, in spite of the frugal habits of a lifetime, the
family savings were not large. Fortunately, his long service and
high earnings combined to produce a dismissal wage of about
$1700, a sum large enough to maintain the family standard of
living for a considerable period of time. Immediately after the
shutdown he succeeded in finding other work but his earnings
were barely one-half what they had been at the plant. His first
son also succeeded in finding a job. He, too, had steady work
but had only about two-thirds his former earnings. The net
result was that a reduced income, coupled with heavy medical
expense, had forced the family to draw upon the dismissal wage
fund for current expenses.

In the course of the interview the families were asked how
much of their dismissal wage payment was still available.
Doubtless there was a certain amount of inaccuracy in the answers; the tendency to exaggerate was undoubtedly strong in a
number of cases. At any rate only 26 out of 90 dismissal wage
families surveyed reported having any of their dismissal wages

left. The typical proportion still remaining seemed to be about one-half, with only four workers admitting that none of it had yet been touched. Two of these were women with payments of about $200 each; the other two were men who had received $1100 and $1500 respectively. A rough estimate indicates that approximately one-fifth of the $47,212 paid to these 90 workers was still available in liquid form at the end of a year. Most of the money was used to tide the workers and their families over a period of adjustment.

With a view to determining the adequacy of these payments for such a purpose, the following table has been constructed. The question has been phrased as follows: To what extent did the dismissal wage payments cover the losses in earning power in the year following the shutdown? It has been brought out in the preceding section that practically all classes of workers suf-

TABLE 16

Annual Earnings, Dismissal Wage Workers, New Haven

Showing percentage comparisons with 1928 earnings of (1) 1929–30 earnings, and (2) 1929–30 earnings plus dismissal wage payments; by sex and age groups

	MEN			WOMEN		
AGE GROUPS	Number of Workers Reporting Comparable Data	1929–30 Earnings (1928 = 100%)	1929–30 Earnings Plus Dismissal Wage Payment (1928 = 100 %)	Number of Workers Reporting Comparable Data	1929–30 Earnings (1928 = 100%)	1929–30 Earnings Plus Dismissal Wage Payment (1928 = 100%)
Total	*53*	*40.2%*	*83.9%*	*20*	*36.3%*	*82.0%*
30–34	1	16.0	54.3	1	14.5	36.5
35–39	3	48.3	83.5	2	31.5	73.3
40–44	4	73.0	113.3	4	54.9	102.4
45–49	16	42.3	79.6	8	25.8	66.1
50–54	16	29.3	68.9	4	53.0	122.4
55–59	11	32.5	94.4	1	9.5	40.7
60–64	2	76.2	136.7	0	...	...

fered heavy reductions in earnings after the shutdown. Those receiving dismissal wages suffered more than the average, largely because they were in the older age groups. The problem is whether the dismissal wages were adequate to carry them at their previous standard of living for a period of one year, by supplementing their earnings in their new jobs.

The extremely heavy losses in earning power of both men and

women is shown in the table. Thus 1929–30 earnings for the
men barely exceeded 40 per cent of 1928 while for women the
proportion was only 36 per cent. Adding to these 1929–30
earnings the total amount of dismissal wages received by these
same workers has the effect of cutting the losses very considerably but leaves them still significant. The essential similarity
in the percentages for men and women (84 *versus* 82) indicates
that it was not a matter of sex. For the most part, also, the
final result is quite independent of age, due to the fact that,
although earnings were lower for the oldest workers, at the same
time the dismissal wage payments were higher because of long
service. However, because of the small numbers involved, the
data for particular age groups are generally erratic.

III. THE FAMILY IN UNEMPLOYMENT

The 672 scheduled New Haven workers, when duplicate members of the same family were eliminated, represented 606 households or family groups. This duplicate 11 per cent does not by any means measure the volume of family relationships existing among the working force in the L. Candee plant. In the above analysis only those workers living in the same household with another worker were rated as duplicate members of the family; no allowance was made for mere kinship between families. Had there been any way of tracing down the full volume of family relationships existing in the plant they would have been found to be of wide extent.

On the other hand, family relationships in the Hartford plant were at a minimum. The fact that only 534 individuals out of more than 1100 could be located for interviewing purposes is ample evidence of the lack of settled family life among these men. Furthermore, those who were found and interviewed would naturally be the more stable group of workers; the unattached single men living in rooming houses had moved away by the time the survey began. Therefore, the 534 who were interviewed did not constitute a good sample of the entire plant. However, the data for these men does throw light upon the status of family life among the established Hartford residents.

Not only were the workers in Hartford more difficult to locate for survey purposes, but even when found they were more reluctant to give information on family affairs. They were on the whole a more highly skilled, higher-wage group, whose social status was appreciably higher than that of the New Haven workers. Consequently 128 schedules (out of the 534 obtained), which were quite satisfactory for job experience data, had to be dropped in the family analysis. There remained only 406 schedules covering 400 families, for which the family data could be tabulated.

The marked difference between the workers in the two cities is shown by the extent of family duplication in the schedules.

While nearly 11 per cent of the families in New Haven had duplicate members working in the plant, less than 2 per cent of the Hartford families were in the same position.

As noted previously, the New Haven work force was divided 45 per cent—55 per cent into foreign-born and native-born. However, the majority of these native-born were simply the first-generation descendants of foreign-born immigrants, only one-seventh (8½ per cent of the total force) being native Americans of at least two generations. In view of the strong ties of family, language and customs existing between these first-generation children and their foreign-born parents, it has been considered more fruitful for the purpose of this study to rate these native-born children as being of the same nationality as their parents rather than as Americans. The latter term has been used to cover only native-born children of native-born parents. On the basis of this method of classification the accompanying table shows the contrast between the nationality composition of the working forces in the two plants.

TABLE 17

Nationality of Heads of Families Reporting Satisfactory Family Data

NATIONALITY	NUMBER OF FAMILIES		PERCENTAGES OF TOTAL	
	New Háven	Hartford	New Háven	Hartford
Total	*606*	*400*	*100.0*	*100.0*
American	52	122	8.6	30.5
White	49	105	8.1	26.2
Colored	3	17	.5	4.3
Italian	350	60	57.8	15.0
Polish	62	57	10.2	14.2
Irish	45	35	7.6	8.8
Lithuanian	26	11	4.4	2.7
German	25	3	4.1	0.8
Canadian	7	46	1.2	11.5
French	5	28	.8	7.0
Other	2	18	.3	4.5
All Other	39	66	6.4	16.5

In New Haven the Americans constituted only a small proportion of the total families (considerably less than one-tenth). The Italians were the predominant nationality, accounting for nearly 58 per cent, and when the Polish group is added, the proportion for these two together amounts to more than two-thirds of all the families. The Canadians, whether French or other, constituted only about 1 per cent of the total.

In Hartford the situation was quite different. When these workers were classified on the nationality basis outlined above, the native-born Americans of two generations formed nearly 30 per cent of the total. This means that only about one-third of the native-born were the first-generation descendants of foreigners, as contrasted with six-sevenths of the New Haven native-born.

The difficulties of coverage involved in the survey resulted in some marked difference in the proportions of the various nationalities, as compared with the total number of families. The Americans, both white and colored, were represented to just about the right extent. The Italians, Poles, Irish, Lithuanians, and Canadians other than French all turned out to be over-represented in the 400 families, while French Canadians, Germans, and All Others were under-represented, the first two very much so.

In order to discover if this shortage of certain nationalities was likely to affect the family data to any appreciable extent, the results of certain tabulations were classified on a nationality basis. It was found that for (1) the number of persons in the family, (2) the number of wage-earners in the family, (3) home ownership and (4) amount of illness in the family, nationality makes some difference. Specifically, the under-representation of the French Canadians probably affects all the general averages for the Hartford group.

In certain other respects the under-representation of the French-Canadians and the loss of the single men operate in the same direction, i. e., cumulatively. This applies in the case of home ownership. The French-Canadians, even those who were family men, were far below average in owning their homes. But, in addition, single men would not be home owners anyway. Hence, there is little doubt that the home ownership percentage for Hartford is somewhat too high either (1) for the entire force at the plant, or even (2) for the family men only.

SIZE AND COMPOSITION OF FAMILY GROUPS

The internal structure of the families, or, as they might better be termed, households, varied widely. A classification of these households was made as follows:

(1) Single individuals—men or women living by themselves, in the sense that they shared no family responsibilities with the people with whom they lived or from whom they rented a room. These workers were not necessarily "single" as to marital status—some of them had been married and had reared families—but for various reasons they were now living alone.

(2) Husband and wife only—no children or relatives.

(3) Husband and/or wife with children, but with no others.

(4) Husband and wife, or husband, wife and children, plus additional members such as grandparents, married children (who would really then form part of a new family), or other relatives. Roomers or boarders living with the family on a purely commercial basis, and not being related to any member of the family in any way, were not counted.

(5) Households of non-marital relationships—brothers and sisters only, an aunt and a niece, etc.

The following table shows how the households were divided between these five classes:

TABLE 18

Number of Families by Classes of Households

CLASS	NUMBER OF FAMILIES	
	New Haven	Hartford
Total	*606*	*400*
1 Single Individuals	31	36
2 Husband and wife only	60	46
3 Husband and/or wife with children	399	254
4 Husband and/or wife with children plus other relatives	91	60
5 Non-marital relationships	20	2
Unknown Composition	5	2

The basic fact emphasized by the table is the predominance of the "natural family"—using that term to represent classes 2 and 3, which cover the family proper in the narrow sense. In almost two-thirds of all cases the household consisted of the husband and/or wife with children, while an additional 10 per cent of the total were composed of the husband and wife only. Thus, in both plants, at least three-quarters of the households comprised normal families, with no outsiders present. Another additional fraction of the total consisted of isolated single individuals. When these three classes are accounted for, there remain the households of complex family relationships comprising less than 20 per cent of the whole number. That is, about one household in five simulates the old clan or family group with its multiplicity of cross-relationships.

In New Haven there were 91 households in which the natural family had appendages of various kinds in the form of more or less distant relatives. Aged dependent relatives, such as parents or grandparents, constitute an important group of this type. Sometimes this is simply a family within a family, as when married sons and daughters live with their parents. In other cases, the relationship of the additional members is more remote; cousins, nephews, nieces, and, of course, many in-laws are to be found in this group. There were 20 households in which strictly non-marital relationships existed. For the most part, these were brothers and sisters who had never married; but, in addition, there were other types of relationship of a much more distant sort. In the Hartford group there were only 2 households of this type.

THE FAMILY'S WAGE EARNERS

The next step is to note the way in which the structure of the family (or household) is related to the economic life of the community. Few indeed were the families in this group who could count upon any substantial independent means of support apart from the job. Incomes of these families were derived almost entirely from the earnings of wage workers, and therefore the key to the family economic status must be found in the quality and quantity of wage earners available to it. Sometimes the household was well supplied with wage earners, as when three or four out of five adults in a given household were holding jobs, but occasionally there came to light a case of, let us say, a family with six or eight children in which the husband was the *only* wage earner. The table shows the general status of the households with respect to the number of wage earners.

The table brings out a number of points of great significance. Of particular importance is the record of the married couples

without children.   Out of 120 members of such families in New
Haven, there were 113 wage earners, which means that only
seven wives were not working.   These couples were scattered
through all age groups, but were especially numerous in the 20's
and 30's.   But of the seven couples in which the wife was not
working, four were above 50 years of age.   Among the young
people the wife was practically always a wage-earning partner,
at least up until the time she had children.   Such figures as these
deal a rather heavy blow to the popular notion that marriage
means the end of the industrial career of a working-class woman.

TABLE 19

Size of Household and Number of Wage Earners

	NEW HAVEN		HARTFORD	
	Average No. of Persons	Average No. of Wage Earners	Average No. of Persons	Average No. of Wage Earners
All Households (excluding unknown)..	4.8	2.4	4.3	1.6
Single Individuals	1.0	1.0	1.0	1.0
Husband and Wife only..............	2.0	1.9	2.0	1.3
Husband and/or Wife and Children...	5.5	2.6	5.0	1.6
Husband and/or Wife and Children and other Relatives.................	5.4	2.5	4.8	2.2
Non-marital	3.0	2.2	3.0	2.0

The data for the fourth group emphasize a slightly different
point, namely, that in these cases the household represents a
judicious mixture of dependent and wage-earning relatives.   If
the "natural" family, which is the base of the combination, is
doing well, aged and dependent relatives seem to flock in, and
may be found in considerable numbers attached to the household.   On the other hand, if the family is doing badly they try
to bring in wage-earning relatives who will pay board and rent,
and who may be induced to contribute directly to the family
budget.   In Hartford especially the high proportion of wage
earners in this group is very striking.

The difference between the social status and standards of living of the families in the two cities is clearly set forth in the data.
Not only were the New Haven families larger, but they had
many more wage earners in proportion to their size.   The average number of wage earners per family exceeded the number in

Hartford in the ratio of 3 to 2, while the proportion of wage earners to total persons in the family was 50 per cent in New Haven and only 37 per cent in Hartford. The average number of wage earners per family[1] for the United States, according to the United States Census of 1930, is about 1.8. Thus the New Haven families are far above average and Hartford slightly below. Note the much higher proportion of working wives in New Haven, as shown by the data for groups two and three.

THE FAMILY ECONOMY

In the analysis of these families certain basic facts concerning the family mode of living come to attention at once. The most important one involved the housing arrangements, since this influences eventually all the conditions under which the family lives. The first table shows the degree of home ownership existing among these families.

TABLE 20

Home Ownership

	New Haven	Hartford
Total Families	606	400
Families Owning Home	210	79
Families Not Owning Home	370	292
Families—Ownership Unknown	26	29

Home Ownership

Thus, approximately one-third of all New Haven families had the ownership of the home vested somewhere in the family. This does not mean that in every case the ownership was vested in the ex-Candee worker or his immediate family; sometimes it might lie with the grandparents on either side, or even with some other relative living with the family. But even these qualifications are of minor importance, since less than 10 per cent of the home owners were other than members of the immediate family.

Among the 400 families which furnished satisfactory family data in Hartford, only 79 owned their homes. Thus, despite

[1] The census definition of a " family " differs from that used here in that the term as used in the census includes *all* persons living under the same roof and eating at a common table. Thus a family would include commercial boarders and roomers.

the generally higher standard of living of the Hartford workers, the proportion of home ownership was very much less—only about 20 per cent of the families being home owners as compared with nearly 35 per cent in New Haven. Further analysis indicates that nationality differences may have had a bearing on this. Home ownership among Irish and Italians was high and among French Canadians very low; the two former nationalities were prominent in New Haven, the latter in Hartford.

Nothing in this study itself is directed toward the problem of home ownership in working-class families, but the question of the desirability of such ownership could scarcely help but obtrude itself into the investigation. Is home ownership a desirable thing for wage-earning families and should it be urged upon them? Or should it rather be discouraged? The arguments in favor of home ownership are too well known to need elaboration—the incentive to saving, the increase in stability, and the enhancement of prestige and standing in the community, are among the many valid reasons for the worker's investment in a home. There is the further fact that most industrial workers are not adept in investing in securities or intangibles; they want to have visible proof that they have bought something, and their judgment in respect to homes is undoubtedly much better than would be the case in the purchase of securities or the choice of a bank. Nevertheless, home ownership does involve certain disabilities which are all too patent in this particular situation.

In the first place, it very decidedly limited the mobility of the worker and his family. Workers who might readily have accepted transfer to other cities felt that they could not leave their homes; had they been renting they would have felt no such compunction. A specific instance of this occurred in the case of the 75 workers who were offered a transfer to the Naugatuck plant of the United States Rubber Company some time after the New Haven plant had been shut down. It had been found that a certain type of worker was needed at Naugatuck and a letter was sent out to the former New Haven workers who might qualify. Out of 75 individuals only 4 replied expressing interest in the possibility. During the field work on this study a special effort was made to find out why the workers failed to respond.

For those workers who were unemployed at the time the invitation came, it was found that the prevailing reason was inability of the family to move. Thus a young girl could not go because the family could not leave New Haven, where the father may have had a job, for example. There were, likewise, some cases of workers who simply did not want to leave their accustomed haunts, even for the sake of a job. On the other hand, there were cases where the responsible head of the family had to refuse transfer because he was unable to move to Naugatuck, and frequently the ownership of the home was given as the reason for this inability. In Hartford the Rubber Company undertook part of the responsibility for disposing of the homes of workers who accepted transfer to the Detroit factory.

There is the still further fact that while home ownership may be eminently desirable so long as the wage earners are employed and the family is prosperous, it has its weaknesses in times of adversity. Mortgage payments fall due and must be met under the most difficult family circumstances. Although only a handful of these families had as yet lost their homes through foreclosures and sheriffs' sales, a considerable number were in arrears in payments and were apprehensive of the outcome. Furthermore, a home is not a highly liquid investment on which ready cash can easily be obtained. With the advent of depression the selling value shrinks badly, and it is the owner's equity which absorbs the entire shrinkage. Under these circumstances it is practically impossible for a family to raise any ready cash on the home, even after years of payments. We found families living in absolute destitution in homes valued at thousands of dollars but on which it seemed to be impossible to realize anything. At least the family could think of no way to do it.

One big advantage obtained by the home owner was security of tenure—he did not have to face eviction upon default of one payment, as the renter had to do. As a matter of fact, however, landlords were frequently lenient, and would permit unpaid rent to accumulate for some months without taking action looking toward eviction, so that this danger was often for the renter more apparent than real.

It is of interest to note the extent of the rent burden. The following table shows the monthly payments of the New Haven families who furnished data on amount of rent paid. The single individuals are separated from the others because their payments are mostly for furnished rooms:

TABLE 21

New Haven Families Classified by Amount of Rent Paid

| | NUMBER OF FAMILIES | |
MONTHLY RENT PAYMENTS	Families of Two or More Members	Single Individuals
Total	*336*	*34*
$50 and over..................................	1	..
45–49	4	..
40–44	6	..
35–39	10	..
30–34	25	..
25–29	76	3
20–24	70	3
15–19	88	5
Below $15	35	13
Unknown	21	10

These rents do not appear to be unduly high, even for working-class families. Only 11 families were paying $40 or more, and less than 15 per cent of those reporting were paying $30 and up. The median falls exactly in the middle of the $20–$24 class, and thus averages out at $22.50. The arithmetic mean of the series is $21.93. This is not an exorbitant figure in the light of the family incomes of these workers. On the basis of the arithmetic mean, the annual rent would be $263, or almost exactly $5 per week. For an average Candee family of 2 wage earners (a man and a woman), earning regular Company wages, the weekly earnings would have been $31.42 for the men and $20.65 for the women—a total of about $52, of which the rent payments would form only 10 per cent.

In Hartford the rents were appreciably higher, the arithmetic mean being $26.54 per month—about $4.50 above the New Haven average. There were in Hartford many more examples of houses being rented at $40, $50 and up. There is no doubt that the housing standards there were considerably above those in New Haven.

Naturally, there were wide individual differences between families. Some were paying entirely too little for their needs;

others were spending more than what was necessary or desirable in the circumstances. Nor can the table take any account of quality, although efforts were made by the field workers to get some estimate of the rating of the premises in terms of an average standard. It was found that, despite the poor housing conditions existing in the neighborhood of the Candee factory, a majority of the families lived there, mostly in tenement apartments. On the other hand, some families had the good sense to move out into the suburbs where it was possible to get a comfortable house and a small lot for as low as $20 to $25 per month, a place which gave them a standard of living far above that existing in the congested city areas. It was the clannishness and close family ties of certain nationalities which kept them clustered in compact neighborhoods. The Americans and the older immigrant nationalities such as Irish, Germans, etc., had moved out to the better neighborhoods. The Italians and Poles, for the most part, lived under slum conditions in the center of the city. This was almost wholly a matter of deliberate choice. There was, for example, no problem of transportation which rendered close residence necessary; street cars ran regularly and the trip to outlying sections of the city was not a long one.

Illness

One great emergency which hangs continually over the heads of the industrial worker's family is that of illness, either of the chief wage earner or of some other member. These families were asked to report upon cases of serious illness or accident which had occurred in the family in the interval since the plant had closed. "Serious" was interpreted to mean, for a wage earner, loss of time sufficient to cause rather heavy loss of income (say at least $50), and for another member of the family illness involving hospitalization, special nursing, or substantial doctor bills. Thus a minor cold causing a few days' loss of time would not count, nor would whooping cough among the children. The table shows the figures on illness.

These cases of illness must either have occurred for the first time, or, if they were previous cases, must have had serious repercussions during this period. Thus, a tuberculosis case in which the patient was still in a sanitarium would be counted. On the other hand, the presence in the family of a permanent cripple who required no medical attention would not be counted, nor would aged dependents.

TABLE 22

Families Reporting Serious Illness or Accident in the Family in the Interval
Since the Shutdown

	New Haven	Hartford
Total	*606*	*400*
Families Experiencing Illness of some Member........	153	97
Families Reporting no Illness......................	428	199
Families—Illness Unknown	25	104

In this particular case it seems reasonably safe to assume that the vast majority of the "unknown" were actually cases of "no illness." Interpreting the illness cases on this basis we find that almost exactly one-fourth of each group reported illness during the period. In approximately two-thirds of the cases a wage earner was afflicted; in the remainder, some other members of the family. These figures seem to indicate that wage earners suffer out of all proportion to their numbers, since they comprise on the average only two persons out of five. For the most part this is true in that wage earners are the only ones affected by industrial accidents.

The additional exaggeration of wage earners' illnesses is probably due to the fact that for these persons it means not only a large financial outlay for medical care, but also a heavy loss of income. Two weeks in bed for a $30 a week wage earner is something for the family to think about; for one of the children it might not even be remembered.

An attempt was made in the course of the study to get data on the costs of illness, both in terms of expense and also of lost income, but this proved to be impracticable. Many times the families did not know how much they owed the doctor. The amount is immaterial if it cannot be paid anyway, so the doctor doesn't bother to send a bill. He takes what they can give and calls it square. Loss of income could be estimated fairly accurately if the length of time away from the job could be determined, but many workers could not remember very well how long they had been out. The result was that it was quite impossible to make any estimate of the total cost of medical care for these families.

One point is quite clear. If it were not for workmen's compensation for accidents, free clinics, city hospitals, and underpaid doctors, these families could not possibly command sufficient medical care for their families, even according to present standards. (That the present medical care is quite inadequate needs no argument.[1]) Some idea of the extremely high cost of serious illness for families who pay their full way may be obtained from the following cases.

One was that of a man whose wife was so ill that a full time nurse was required at a cost of $7 per day, which was considerably more than the husband himself was earning. But when he attempted to stay home to take care of his sick wife, his job with the railroad company was threatened, so that he had to take the more expensive course. At the time of the field worker's visit, despite the tremendous debt burden that was piling up, the husband refused to have a family relief society notified of the case. It was only through a hint to the Visiting Nurse Association that contact was made with the family and the proper moves taken to save the husband from complete financial disaster.

Another case was that of a highly-skilled workman who had a long record of service at the plant. He owned his home (a fine house in the outskirts of the city), his son worked at the plant, the family had savings at the bank. But another son was a helpless cripple requiring constant medical care and attention. In the period following the shutdown special efforts were required. This man estimated that he had paid out over a period of a few years about $3000 for the care of his crippled son. For that family, illness was threatening the savings of a lifetime.

Insurance Coverage

The extent to which these families were covered by insurance is very striking. Even the poorest families were heavily insured. In both places barely one-eighth of the families reported no

---

[1] See Peebles, Allon, *A Survey of the Medical Facilities of the State of Vermont*, The Committee on the Costs of Medical Care, Washington, D. C., 1932.

TABLE 23

Number of Families Covered by Insurance

INSURANCE STATUS	NUMBER OF FAMILIES	
	New Haven	Hartford
Total	606	400
Families Carrying Insurance	478	227
Families Not Insured...............................	76	51
Insurance Unknown	52	122

insurance carried on any member of the family, although some of the unknowns unquestionably belonged in this group. However, it is clear that probably around 80–85 per cent of all families carried some insurance. The uninsured families were by no means the poorest of the group. Although, when questioned as to the reasons for not having insurance, they frequently gave as an excuse the argument that "they weren't able to afford it," in actual fact they were generally small families or single individuals who had no dependents, and in many cases they were far better off financially than families insured up to the limit.

A better idea of the volume of insurance carried by these families can be obtained from the extent of coverage in individual families. The next table shows these figures for those families reporting insurance:

TABLE 24

Extent of Coverage in Insured Families

COVERAGE	NUMBER OF FAMILIES	
	New Haven	Hartford
Total	478	227
All Members Insured...............................	314	105
Some Members Insured, but not All.................	145	113
Coverage Unknown	19	9

When all members are insured, it means not just adults but every child as well. There were families of 9, 10, 12 or more members, every one of whom had some insurance, even though it might be only a $100 policy. When not all members are insured it does not mean that the family is not carrying a lot of insurance. Most families in this latter group had a majority of the members covered; it was a rarity to find one in which only the chief wage earner carried insurance. Generally, it was one or two younger children who were not covered; wives were almost invariably insured, and of course the husband, too.

The New Haven workers appear to have gone in for insurance more wholeheartedly than those in Hartford, which is a little surprising in view of the reputation of the latter as the "insurance city of America." This is all the more surprising in that these Hartford workers were on a higher wage level and had a better standard of living than the New Haven group. Nevertheless, two-thirds of the New Haven families had all members insured while in Hartford the proportion was less than half.

Finally there is still a third way of expressing the insurance coverage—in terms of the premium payments. The table shows these payments reduced to a common weekly basis.

TABLE 25

Equivalent Weekly Premium-Payments on Insurance Carried

WEEKLY PREMIUM PER FAMILY	NUMBER OF FAMILIES		PER CENT OF TOTAL FAMILIES	
	New Haven	Hartford	New Haven	Hartford
Total	478	227	100.0	100.0
$6.00 and over............	11	2	2.3	0.9
5.00–5.99	18	4	3.8	1.8
4.00–4.99	27	6	5.6	2.6
3.00–3.99	56	19	11.7	8.3
2.00–2.99	82	40	17.2	17.6
1.00–1.99	135	72	28.2	31.9
0.00–0.99	83	56	17.4	24.6
Amount Unknown.........	66	28	13.8	12.3

At $3.00 per week and up, New Haven families were nearly twice as numerous proportionately as Hartford families—nearly one-fourth of the whole group were in these premium classes as against less than one-seventh of those in Hartford. On the other hand in premium classes under $3.00 per week the latter were considerably in excess of New Haven, particularly in the class under $1.00. The difference is even more clearly expressed in the arithmetic means, which were $2.27 per family for New Haven as compared with $1.83 for Hartford. Converted to a yearly basis these figures become $118 and $95 respectively, which indicate that insurance payments were averaging about 5–10 per cent of total family income. There were cases of families paying from $6–$8 per week for insurance—premiums which would amount to $300–$400 per year, a wholly impossible burden for families with these incomes. One family was paying $8.15 a week out of a total maximum family income of about $58 per week; another was insured to the extent of $9.00 on an income of $68.50; a third reported the incredible sum of $12 per week in insurance payments on an income of $77. Furthermore, these were prosperity incomes; the unemployment of the Candee rubber worker laid off in the shutdown had already affected these incomes adversely. They had all three fallen—to $54, $47.50, and $51 respectively.

The most discouraging feature of the whole situation was not so much the amounts being paid in, as it was the kind of insurance held. For the most part, the insurance was of the industrial type, that is, paid by the week rather than quarterly or annually. This type of insurance involves heavy collection charges, and for that reason the premiums are appreciably higher than for ordinary insurance. Of course, the argument is made that these people cannot save up to make the longer-term payments, whereas they can be impelled to set aside a certain amount each week. But, whatever the cause, it is clear that for the money expended the worker is getting comparatively little insurance. And there is the further disadvantage that industrial policies have little or no loan or cash-surrender value, thus making it impossible for the family to realize anything in times of distress. Under these circumstances insurance has no value at all as savings.

The fact that industrial policies are available in very small amounts encourages the indiscriminate insurance of all members of the family at a rather high cost. A child of five is insured as heavily as the head of the family. A great deal of the insurance on the children is nothing more than "burial" insurance. It is in no sense a protection for dependents when the insured is not, and will not for many years, be a wage earner contributing to the support of the family. If the youngster dies, the funeral expenses can be paid out of the insurance, and in practically all cases the entire amount is thus expended. The tenacity with which the families cling to this type of insurance is illustrated by several cases in which the pressure of unemployment and reduced incomes forced the dropping of several policies; in practically all these families, it was the father's and mother's policies which were dropped, while the children's were kept. Generally, this was because the latter were much cheaper and could be kept up after the heavier payments on the older policies had to be given up. Nevertheless, it is a commentary on the role played by insurance in family life that its function should become so distorted.

So far as the period of unemployment is concerned, there is little evidence that it brought severe pressure on the insurance payments. There were isolated cases of insurance policies being dropped, but they were so few as to be insignificant. On the other hand, there is plenty of evidence at hand to indicate that the insurance is carried, even at the cost of food and other necessaries. The landlord might often be some months behind in his rent, but not a single one of the insurance policies had been disturbed. Of course that could not be kept up indefinitely, and had the study been continued into the second winter of unemployment, it is more than likely that many cases of dropped and surrendered policies would have been found. Nevertheless, it is clear that the workers cling to the insurance as long as they can, and give it up only as a last resort; sometimes they actually go on charity carrying the full complement of insurance policies.

Debts

When other resources became exhausted, families found it necessary to make use of their credit, if any. In the survey they were asked what debts they had contracted; what loans they had made. The table shows the number reporting such indebtedness.

The proportion of families contracting debts was just 11 per cent in New Haven and 17 per cent in Hartford. The excess in the latter place was probably a reflection of the higher wages and better credit standing of that group. The relative debt status of the two groups is probably fairly well expressed by the figures. However, it is certain that neither figure adequately measures the situation. Information of this sort was difficult to get and the tendency of the family to conceal financial troubles was rather marked in some instances. But at least we have here recorded the very minimum number of families who had had to resort to credit on a large scale in order to tide themselves over the unemployment period.

TABLE 26

Families Contracting Debts

DEBT STATUS	NUMBER OF FAMILIES	
	New Haven	Hartford
Total	*606*	*400*
Families contracting debts...........................	67	67
Families having no debts.............................	498	193
Families—debts unknown	41	140

The interpretation of this question was very strict. The object was to get data on commercial loans, whether obtained from commercial banks, private banks, mutual loan associations, small loan companies, Morris Plan banks, or from friends and relatives (so long as the loan was on a commercial basis). The loan from a friend or relative had to be substantial in amount, and scheduled for repayment, in order to qualify. The borrowing of large amounts, say several hundred dollars, from one's father would be classified under the head of "help from relatives" rather than as a loan, since it is doubtful if full repayment would be expected. Merchant credit caused the most difficulty. A small charge account at a neighborhood store was not considered the equivalent of commercial indebtedness, but when the bill had run for some months and totaled some hundred dollars or more, then it clearly came in that class. So with back rent owed to the landlord. In the final counting these two forms of credit were charged against the family only when they had reached substantial amounts. Therefore, the figures recorded in the table are far from measuring the number of families who had obtained credit. The count includes only those who had done so on a sufficiently large scale to make it a serious family problem.

There was no prevailing method of getting credit. The small loan companies, with their 3½ per cent interest per month, were sporadically used, but so were the Morris Plan banks, and there were even occasional commercial banks. But generally the source of a loan was either long-extended merchant credit or friends. Apparently among the Italians in New Haven there are a great number of free-lance lenders who operate without license and without supervision. Their interest charges are fantastic, since they are free from any restrictions, and their victims never come into court. The extent of this kind of lending is impossible to estimate, but that it exists on a wide scale is beyond question.

One point of considerable interest is the large volume of credit obtained. Once a family begins borrowing, they continue to expand to the limit. It is such an easy method, and the penalty is light. There was the case of a family which contracted loans to the extent of $1700 in the short space of six or eight months, the weekly repayments on which amounted to $35 per week. This was actually greater than the total weekly income of the family at the time of the investigator's visit. It was utterly impossible for this family to pay back the loans that they had obtained from half a dozen different sources, mostly small loan companies.

Charitable Help

The complete list of the Candee workers was cleared through the Social Service Exchange operated by the New Haven Community Chest. The Exchange report showed that out of 662 families representing the 729 workers in the plant, 206 were known to the regular social agencies. This in itself gives some indication of the large volume of social work which had been done for these families. However the registrations themselves are not all of equal significance; many involved nothing more than a visit to the hospital dispensary or treatment by the Visiting Nurse Association. Also, many of these registrations dated back many years and were of no significance for purposes of this survey. The accompanying table gives a clearer picture of the charity record of these families than the total figures themselves can give.

Approximately one-third of the families known to social agencies had been registered with relief organizations as distinct from such non-relief organizations as hospitals, visiting nurses, visiting

TABLE 27

Welfare Record of Candee Families Known to Social Agencies

TIME PERIOD	No. of Families	Relief Organ.	Non-Relief Organ. Only
Total	*206*	*66*	*140*
Since April, 1929, only..............	19	8	11
Both since and prior to April, 1929..	24	12	12
Prior to April, 1929, only...........	163	46	117

teachers, etc. The second point of interest is that although nearly a year had elapsed since the shutdown in April, 1929, the vast majority of these families had not been registered since that time. Only 8 families became known to relief organizations for the first time and only 12 more with previous records had had to come back. This makes a total of 20 families among the Candee workers who applied for relief in the one year following the shutdown. The figures indicate that charitable relief played a very small part in aiding these families over their period of unemployment.

IV. JOB HUNTING IN HARD TIMES

To the extent that the Candee shutdown was timed at all by the Company, the date was set in the expectation that the usual seasonal Spring upturn in employment would provide for the ready absorption of the displaced workers. There were two independent possibilities in this direction: industrial employment might be expanding, and in any case agricultural jobs would be opening up. It is necessary to examine the Company's theory on this point in the light of actual results.

First, as to industrial employment, the prospective seasonal expansion did not occur. The following table shows the variation in employment and man-hours of operation of 65 factories in the city of New Haven over the period under consideration.

TABLE 28

Employment and Man-Hours in 65 New Haven Factories*

(Monthly, Jan., 1929–June, 1930)

Month	Number of Employes	Man-Hours (in Millions of Labor–Hours)
1929 Jan.	23,688	5.15
Feb.	23,956	4.64
Mar.	23,766	4.69
Apr.	23,609	4.93
May	23,356	4.78
June	23,396	4.70
July	22,613	4.54
Aug.	23,180	4.62
Sept.	23,030	4.48
Oct.	22,835	4.98
Nov.	22,399	4.47
Dec.	21,706	4.11
1930 Jan.	21,491	4.38
Feb.	21,083	4.02
Mar.	21,025	4.05
Apr.	21,808	4.16
May	20,525	3.86
June	19,801	3.53

* By courtesy of the secretary, New Haven Chamber of Commerce.

These figures, although they do not include all factories in the city, represent a fairly complete coverage of industrial New Haven. The United States Census of 1930 shows that out of 69,256 gainfully employed people in the city of New Haven approximately 30,000 were strictly industrial, of whom about 23,000 were men and 7,000 women. Altogether about 800 workers (including foremen and minor officials) were laid off in the Candee shutdown. This number constituted less than 3 per cent of the total industrial wage-earning population of the city. In other words, on a comparative basis the problem of reabsorption of these workers was not an especially large one.

The chief difficulty was, as the table shows, that the volume of industrial employment in New Haven had been declining since early in the year and continued to decline throughout the period between the shutdown and the making of the survey (the data for the Candee plant both before and after the shutdown have been eliminated from the above figures). It is necessary to read both columns in order to obtain a reasonably clear picture of what was happening. Employment and man-hours do not always vary in the same direction. This is due to the nature of the figures themselves. Employment represents the number of men on the payroll, which might remain fairly constant even with a considerable reduction in working time. Employers might cut the working hours in preference to laying any men off. On the other hand, the man-hours reflect to some extent the number of working days in the month, so that long months, such as October, show an upturn in man-hours when in fact there was an actual decrease in employment, as shown by the employment figures.

For the first six months of their unemployment the Candee workers had a reasonably good chance of getting a job. Barring the usual seasonal relapse in July, employment remained fairly steady from early Spring through the month of September. There was no expansion, but at least the workers had a fair opportunity for placement. In the autumn, however, conditions changed for the worse. Between March, 1929, and March, 1930, for example, employment dropped by more than 2,700 workers, all of whom were additional competitors for jobs alongside the Candee workers. Man-hours in the same period had dropped from 4.69 millions to 4.05 millions. Therefore, those workers who did not succeed in finding a job during the first six months of their unemployment, or who were so unfortunate as to lose their new job after this period, found it increasingly difficult to get work. It is this situation which partly accounts for the rapid falling away in the rate of placement in the later months, as shown in the tables. In conclusion, it must be emphasized that for the first six months at least the Candee applicants were facing fairly normal conditions, and were not handicapped by business depression, as they were later on.

Other outlets, i. e., outlets other than those in industry, were not readily available. These workers were almost exclusively industrial, and they could not easily adapt themselves to other conditions. A very few of the young workers succeeded in retraining themselves for clerical or commercial jobs, but these were the exceptional minority. Beth Lowell had spent practically the whole twelve years of her industrial life at the rubber factory. Immediately following the shutdown she obtained a job in a nearby plant, but the shock of discharge led her to think seriously of her future. Without any further delay, she enrolled in a secretarial school to learn stenography. She had kept this up for over a year and will soon receive her diploma. But for the shock of the closing, she might never have had the initiative to plan out her own future.

An even more striking case of advancement is that of Jane Eudake, to whom the shutdown gave the necessary stimulus for the capitalizing of her latent abilities. In the course of twelve years' industrial experience she had been recognized as a person of more than usual capacity. In fact, the Company at one time had given her a few months' trial as forewoman. She was not successful and, to the satisfaction of the management, asked to be transferred back to her old job at the bench. But at the time of the shutdown the strong recommendation of her employers opened up a new kind of opportunity in a responsible position. In contrast to her old job as an industrial wage earner at about $23 a week, her present position is that of a sales executive at $35 a week. She has not only improved her earnings but has entered into a new world entirely different from that of a factory worker. Her work consists in planning window displays and other matters related to sales promotion.

Several similar cases of transfer from the industrial to the business world could be cited. One girl had changed her name, and was very fearful that her new associates would discover the shameful fact that she had once worked in a factory.

Domestic work was open for those who cared to take it, but the number of women who went into domestic or personal service was insignificant. This was partly because many of them had years of industrial work behind them and therefore could not bring themselves to think in terms of domestic employment with no regular hours and little freedom for recreation. Furthermore, the vast majority were of Italian birth or descent, and nationality, habits or customs practically prohibited them from entering domestic service.

The agricultural outlet, however sound in theory, was without result in actual practice. While a number of men reported having looked for jobs in the farming areas outside New Haven, only one or two found anything which held them for any length of time. The fact is that the men were as averse to agricultural work as the women were to domestic; therefore, comparatively few would have benefited from it, even if it had been available.

Yale University for some years had been engaged on a vast program of physical expansion, resulting in a large volume of building construction for a city the size of New Haven. All during the year following the shutdown the Yale building program had been proceeding at full speed, with the expenditure of millions of dollars in the employment of between one and two thousand men. Nevertheless, it is of interest to report that *not one* of the Candee workers found a job on this construction work (there were several men and two women who obtained jobs on the permanent Yale University force, but this had no connection with the building program). The difficulty was not so much that the workers did not apply for jobs, or that the construction companies would not have been glad to use them, but the unusual character of the construction work was not such as to offer an opportunity for the rubber workers. Most of the Yale buildings were being constructed on a plan which required the materials to be delivered in manufactured form; the construction consisted in large measure of putting blocks of stone in place. It offered no opportunity for carpenters, very little for bricklayers, and comparatively little for the common run of building trades workmen; and there was no place for untrained factory workers.

The result was that the Candee workers had no real opportunities for jobs in any other than the industrial field. Most of those who got jobs obtained them in this field, and those who were not successful went for the most part without work over the entire period. This fact is in itself a commentary on the lack of adaptability of the average industrial worker. Or, to put it a little more accurately, the industrial system is rather sharply sub-divided into different spheres of work, so that it is impractical for a specialized worker in one field to find opportunities in another.

METHODS OF FINDING WORK

In connection with the job history, the worker was asked to state, for each job found during the shutdown period, the method by which he had obtained it. The answer was taken in the worker's own words, but the replies were later classified into certain major groupings. The table below shows the result.

TABLE 29

Successful Methods of Getting Jobs
For 861 jobs obtained by 525 Candee workers

METHOD	Number of Jobs Obtained
Total	*861*
Applied at Plant	391
Help of Friends or Relatives	311
Through Company	73
Newspaper Advertisements	22
Employment Offices	11
Recalled after Layoff	9
Political Influence	6
Miscellaneous	4
Unknown	34

Undoubtedly these data leave much to be desired in accuracy and preciseness. The results must be taken as a rough approximation of conditions in the New Haven labor market and not as a very clear picture. In the first place, a worker may not always know why he got the job; it is of interest that only 73 jobs are reported as being obtained by the Company, although the Company itself reported having placed 175 workers. The difference arises largely out of the point of view. The Company would be inclined to take credit whenever a special letter of recommendation was sent out or a telephone call was made, while the worker might easily ascribe his success to his own application at the plant. There is evidence also that the workers themselves were much impressed with the help given them by friends and relatives. Perhaps in many cases the latter were given credit for the job when their influence was really negligible. Certainly in the workers' minds the Company's efforts were often rated as secondary in comparison with the influence of someone in the plant.

It was frequently somewhat difficult to distinguish between a plant application and the help of friends or relatives. Jobs were not reported as being obtained through help of this kind unless there was definite evidence that it had been effective. For example, workers often heard about a vacancy from someone who already worked in the plant, but the latter did not in any way speak for the applicant or use any influence to get him the job. In that case it was classified as a simple plant application, which accounts for the large number of jobs listed under that heading. Conversely, the 311 jobs attributed to friends and relatives were largely bona fide cases of the use of influence. Such terms as, " Knew the foreman," " Friend spoke for him," " Wife was working there," " Uncle saw employment manager," and so forth, were given. There can be little doubt that the normal method of getting jobs in the city of New Haven is to make application at the plant, supplemented if at all possible by a good word from some friend or relative who already works there.

The chief point of interest about the table is not the leading methods of finding work, but those at the very end of the list. In other words, the methods not tried are fully as significant as those which were used. For example, only 22 reported finding any jobs through newspaper advertisements; most of these were domestic and clerical jobs, only half a dozen were industrial. As for employment offices, they did not even exist for probably 90 per cent of the workers. Many had never even heard of them, and most of those who had heard thought they were of no importance. Of the 11 workers obtaining jobs in this way, 6 got them through private employment agencies on a fee basis, while 4 had been placed through the public employment office, and 1 through the manufacturer's employment office. Political influence appeared in only a few cases; it was apparent that these workers had little political pull. The miscellaneous group consisted of jobs obtained through a priest, a social worker, a lodge and a mission. It is obvious that the New Haven labor market is in no sense organized effectively for placement.

The effect of this disorganization of the labor market upon the workers themselves came to light during the study. Worker after worker reported hunting for jobs by going from plant to plant until he or she became discouraged and decided to wait until times got better. The difficulties of such methods are obvious. The worker can seldom canvass more than one plant a day. He has to be there the first thing in the morning, and if no job is available at that place he hesitates to go anywhere else for fear his late application will be misinterpreted—the employment manager may think he has been sleeping late. On the other hand, it is largely sheer chance that he may happen to be at a plant where a job will open up that morning. Many times, especially among the less highly skilled occupations, the jobs are given to someone who happens to be in the office at the time. Yet the worker cannot hope to be just in the right place at the right time. The discouragement which follows from constant tramping from plant to plant with never a gleam of hope, was eloquently stated by worker after worker. One man, a highly skilled mechanic, furnished the interviewer a list of 53 plants which he had visited in search of a job; the list included practically every metal working plant in the city of New Haven. The irony of it is that the job he finally did obtain came to him, not through his application method at all, but by means of a friend who knew he was looking and got him an opportunity in a plant where the friend was working.

V. SUMMARY

The two United States Rubber Company shutdowns in New Haven and Hartford, accomplished, respectively, in the Spring and Fall of 1929, resulted in the displacement of two representative groups of industrial workers. Despite the marked differences which existed between these two groups, they were fully up to the average of industrial workers in their respective communities. Judged by the standards commonly applied—length of service, wages, efficiency rating, etc.—they were performing their tasks satisfactorily in every sense of the word. The shutdowns were in no way related to the performance of their working force in either plant. These workers, therefore, lost their jobs because of a situation over which they had no control and their unemployment was in no sense a reflection upon their character as workmen. It is for this reason that the survey of their subsequent job experiences is especially valuable. It is a survey of the fortunes of a group of workers recognized in their communities as able men and women.

ANALYSIS OF THE WORKERS

Despite the fact that both working forces were in the employ of the same company and engaged in the same industry, there were marked differences between them—differences so great as to provide sharp contrasts in many important respects. The New Haven plant, being engaged in the manufacture of footwear, found it practicable to employ a large proportion of women; about 60 per cent of the working force were women. On the other hand, the automobile tire manufacturing in Hartford required the use of men almost exclusively, there being only a handful of women in the entire force. In one other respect, also, the differences in the process of manufacture had an effect upon the type of labor employed. Footwear production, up until the time of the shutdown, had remained partly in the handicraft stage, especially in the key process of shoemaking. This made it possible for production operations to be more flex-

ible and individualistic; there was no pressing need for standardi-
zation of processes. In consequence, the labor force had long
had the characteristics of workers adjusted to that type of production method. On the other hand, the manufacture of tires
was a highly mechanized process geared to high speed. Wages
were high but work was hard; and there was no room for loose
or easy-going production methods. The workers, therefore, were
on the whole younger, more vigorous and more highly skilled.

The Candee plant in New Haven was the oldest rubber footwear manufacturing plant in the United States. In view of the
fact that there had been no fundamental changes in process during the past half century, the older workers tended to remain
with the concern. At the time of the closing a considerable proportion of the force were over 45 years of age and quite a number were over 60 years. Long service was the rule among these
older workers, the average length of service of those later given
pensions amounting to nearly 35 years, while for the others over
45 years of age the average service was better than 17 years.
For the entire factory, the length of service, as measured by
total working time, amounted to almost 10 years. Only about
20 per cent of the entire force had worked less than two years.

The Hartford plant was not only much younger, but it had
also undergone revolutionary changes on several occasions. The
change from bicycle tires to automobile tires at about the beginning of the century marked the most important stage of develop-
ment, and the building of the new mechanized factory during
the war marked another stage. Both these changes affected the
quality and character of the working force through rapid expansion as well as through occupational obsolescence. Average service was therefore very much shorter in Hartford; for the entire
plant it was only 5.4 years, slightly more than half that in New
Haven. There was a small proportion of extra-long-service
workers in tire manufacturing, but at the other extreme nearly
40 per cent of the force had less than two years' service. In
further analyzing the workers in the two plants it was found
that these short-service workers in Hartford were largely French
and English-speaking Canadians, who had apparently migrated
to the city during the prosperity period immediately preceding

the shutdown. In New Haven there were only a handful of representatives of these migratory nationalities, the working force being dominated by Italians who were long-time residents of New Haven. The migration was very largely a response to business conditions. The migrants were largely young, unmarried men in the 20's and early 30's. They were not found in the New Haven working force because neither the city nor the plant had been sufficiently prosperous to be attractive.

In the survey the New Haven workers, being residents of long standing in the City, were nearly all located and interviewed; consequently there was no problem of coverage. In Hartford, on the contrary, the migrant workers had nearly all left the City by the time the survey was made and therefore that group was missing in the sample finally obtained. The Hartford data are therefore not wholly representative of the entire working force. On the other hand, since only the more stable workers were included, the group as such were closely comparable to those in New Haven and the possibilities of direct comparison between the two groups actually surveyed are greatly increased thereby. The survey falls short only in that it furnishes no data and justifies no conclusions concerning the younger, migratory workers of certain nationalities who were only temporary residents of Hartford.

Two other factors have an immediate bearing upon the fortunes of the workers after the shutdowns. New Haven, being the first to go, experienced all the difficulties incident to any pioneering job. Mistakes were made, some of which had an influence upon the workers themselves. By contrast, some of the mistakes made in New Haven were obviated in Hartford by a better management of the closing process. The coöperative response of the industrial community in the latter city afforded the workers there a most exceptional opportunity for placement in satisfactory industrial jobs. Against this advantage must be set the disadvantage of the time selected for the shutdown. The New Haven workers had some six months of moderately good business during which to find a new job. The Hartford men scarcely had two months before the full force of industrial depression struck the city and closed many avenues of opportunity to them. Probably these two factors largely counterbalanced each other in the final analysis.

Despite the differences of sex, nationality, length of service, wage rates, etc., between the two working forces, the unemployment experiences of both groups were very much alike. Approximately 30 per cent of the Hartford workers found jobs without appreciable loss of time and nearly 60 per cent were placed within a period of approximately two months. In New Haven nearly 37 per cent were placed without loss of time, while over 63 per cent were placed in approximately two months. These figures show that, in spite of the much more vigorous community action in Hartford, the New Haven workers had a slight advantage in getting work. This was partly due to the more favorable period of the year (March and April), partly to the longer period between the announcement of the shutdown and the final closing, and finally to the better state of business conditions at that time. These impersonal, economic factors proved fully as important as community coöperation and good will in the face of economic difficulties.

Did this first placement solve the worker's problem of readjustment? In many cases it did. Over 57 per cent of the Hartford men who found work at any time were still holding their first job at the time the survey was made. Many of these had gone to the new job without loss of time so that they suffered no unemployment at all as a result of the shutdown. The other 43 per cent lost their first job after varying periods of service. Over half of this group were out of work again within a period of about two months. Many of them succeeded in finding another job and some in turn lost that; 18 workers had held three jobs, 2 had held four and 1 held five during the period between the shutdown and the closing date of the survey.

In New Haven also the first placement was not always permanent, only 46 per cent of those finding work being still in possession of their first job at the close of the survey. Of the others who became unemployed again about one-fifth lost out immediately and considerably more than half were out of work within about two months. There were cases of workers holding as many as six to nine jobs during the period following the shutdown.

The total loss of working time was about the same in both cities. For the entire group who looked for work at all the average time lost by New Haven workers amounted to approximately 40 per cent of the available working time over a period of eleven months. This compared with an average for the Hartford workers of about 43 per cent in a period of ten months.

At the end of the shutdown period, on the closing date of the survey, the great majority of those who had actively sought work were located in a more or less satisfactory job. In Hartford, the proportion at work slightly exceeded 70 per cent of those looking for it; in New Haven the proportion was almost 74 per cent. Some of the others had held jobs during the period but happened to be unemployed as of the closing date.

The total losses suffered by the workers were not fully measured by the amount of unemployment. The vast majority of both men and women suffered sharp cuts in earnings as a result of the change in jobs. Only 9 per cent of the Hartford men who found work at all were able to earn as much on the new job as they had on the old one with the rubber works. On the other hand, over 27 per cent of the New Haven men and women did find new jobs paying at least as high wages as the old. The discrepancy between the two working forces in this respect is largely due to the much higher wage level existing in the Hartford plant.

For the working force as a whole, the loss in earnings was severe. The average weekly earnings of the New Haven men on the best-paid job they were able to obtain after the shutdown barely exceeded 80 per cent of the rubber company rates; the women's losses were even greater, the best-paid job averaging only 76 per cent of the earnings on the old one. The Hartford workers suffered a decline in earnings of nearly 30 per cent, the average on the new job being slightly above 70 per cent of that on the old.

For New Haven a special computation was made of the net effect of unemployment and loss in weekly earnings. The figures show that the total loss in income of the workers in a period of about one year after the shutdown amounted to about 50 per cent of their income during the preceding year with the rubber company. For those workers who received a dismissal wage, these losses were largely made up. For this small special group earnings losses were even more severe than the average; their new earnings averaged less than 40 per cent of the old. The dismissal wage payments brought their total annual income in the year following the shutdown up to more than 83 per cent of their income during the preceding year. Hence the dismissal wage payments fell just short of being sufficient to maintain the worker's income at the old level for a period of one year.

THE FAMILY IN UNEMPLOYMENT

Of those workers surveyed, the typical family relationship was that of a husband and/or wife with children. Very nearly two-thirds of both working forces belonged to families of this type. The addition of couples without children would bring the proportion up to about three-fourths. The remainder were either single individuals living by themselves or members of more complicated family groupings.

The New Haven families averaged somewhat larger than those in Hartford, and their wage earners were very considerably in excess. In general, one member out of every two in the New Haven families was a wage earner. The clearest indication of the marked difference between the living standards in the two cities is given by the families in the husband-wife-children combination. In New Haven, these families averaged 5.5 persons supported by 2.6 wage earners, while in Hartford such families averaged 5.0 persons supported by 1.6 wage earners. Thus the lower earnings of the individual members of that group in New Haven were partly counterbalanced by the income from additional wage earners in the family.

Differences in the methods of earning the family income resulted in marked differences in the family economy. For example, about one family in every three in New Haven owned their home or were at least in the process of purchasing it. In Hartford, only about one family in every five was a home owner.

It must be remembered that these Hartford families were largely the more stable and settled residents of the city. The fact appears to be that home ownership is not correlated very closely with family income. On the other hand, the Hartford families used their higher incomes in renting better houses and apartments. Their average rent amounted to $26.54 per month in comparison with only $21.93 for the renters in New Haven.

The significance of the problem of illness or accident for a working-class family is shown in the figures for both cities. Approximately one-fourth of the families reported cases of serious illness of some member of the family during the period following the shutdown. On this basis the average family would experience a case of serious illness involving either heavy medical expense or loss of income of a wage earning member or both once in every four years.

Insurance was very widely held—about four-fifths of the families in both cities reporting insurance carried on at least one member of the family. Insurance, like home ownership, appears not to be very closely correlated with family income. It was usually the families with higher incomes who did not carry insurance.

Insurance was also widely held within the family. In New Haven over two-thirds of the insured families carried policies on every member of the household, while in Hartford about one-half of the insured families had policies on all members. Generally speaking, the policies on children were very small. Nevertheless, the average cost of insurance per family was $2.27 per week in New Haven and $1.83 in Hartford. Insurance payments averaged about 5 to 10 per cent of total family income.

Some families, either in their normal mode of living or as a result of unemployment after the shutdown, met a part of their difficulties by contracting debts. About 17 per cent of the reporting families in Hartford and 11 per cent of those in New Haven admitted having debts of various kinds. These figures undoubtedly represent a minimum since many families failed to report or would not admit being in debt. Some debts were in the form of commercial loans, others were borrowings from friends or relatives and a considerable amount was represented by merchant credit or back rent to the landlord. Undoubtedly, the use of credit, granted either voluntarily or involuntarily by the creditor, played an important part in carrying some of these families through the unemployment period.

In New Haven only, data on the charity record of these families were obtained from the Social Service Exchange. While a large proportion of these families were known to the regular social agencies (about 30 per cent), only a small number has received any help during the period following the shutdown. Only 20 families had applied for relief at any time during this period. Hence charitable relief was not an important factor in the family economy during the unemployment period.

JOB HUNTING IN HARD TIMES

In their search for work the men and women in New Haven had to rely almost entirely upon old and ineffective methods. In Hartford the community coöperation which was established to aid in the placement resulted in at least a temporary organization and coördination of the labor market for the purpose of locating jobs. But in New Haven such coördination was much less in evidence. The Company was active immediately following the shutdown but outside of that the workers had no help.

The typical methods of looking for work in New Haven are those of applying at the plant or obtaining the aid of friends or relatives working there. In each case this means individual applications at each plant with consequent waste of time to the worker and loss of opportunities through not being in the right place at the right time. A very small proportion of the workers succeeded in finding jobs through newspaper advertisements. Only a fraction made any use of employment offices and the great majority of the workers had never even heard of any such institution.

The shutdown was timed by the Company to catch the usual spring upturn in business, which if it had occurred would have greatly facilitated the industrial readjustments of these workers. However, the data on employment and man-hours in New Haven factories show that there was a more or less steady decline in the number of employes on the payrolls. In the fall of the year the decline became more pronounced and the opportunities for jobs became much smaller.

The records show that these workers found few openings outside the industrial field. The number who succeeded in finding work in the construction industries or in agriculture was so small as to be negligible.

Conclusion

The final results of the study make it clear that the major part of the burden of industrial change, if these two cases are typical, falls upon the workers. Despite the efforts which were made by the Company and by the community in each case, the majority of the workers had to take care of themselves, and suffer whatever losses were involved. Nevertheless, the payment of a dismissal wage to a selected group of workers was of material benefit to them and their families during the readjustment. The results of its use in these two cases were so uniformly good as to justify its extension to other workers and other industries.

For example, there were many workers at both the New Haven and Hartford plants who might well have been entitled to a dismissal wage on the basis of their investment of time and skill with the Company—men and women who fell short of the service required (10 years for workers 45 years and over, and 15 years for others) in order to qualify. A minimum of five years would have brought into the fold a large group of middle-aged and younger workers who were markedly handicapped in making the readjustment. On the other hand, there is every reason for keeping the dismissal wage entirely distinct from unemployment insurance. The former is essentially an indemnity for the probably permanent loss of job and skill, the latter is to cover the temporary readjustment involved in changing jobs. The experiences of the United States Rubber Company workers serve to emphasize the fact that the dismissal wage must take its place as a most important device for the establishment of greater security for the industrial worker.

PART II

FORMER L. CANDEE WORKERS IN THE DEPRESSION

FORMER L. CANDEE WORKERS IN THE DEPRESSION

INTRODUCTORY STATEMENT

The social significance of unemployment is found in the readjustments in living made necessary by the change in work and wage experience; by the change in industrial status involved in the readjustments; and particularly in the cumulative effect of no work as the days and weeks and months of unemployment increase. It is in such facts as these that the lay-off extends its influence into the lives of the families in the community. The decrease in purchasing power, the need for public assistance, and the experiences which make that decrease and that need a permanent possibility are centered here.

Studies of unemployment which picture a cross section of the unemployed on a definite date are limited in the contribution they can make to the outlining of such facts, however valuable they may be in other respects. In order to determine the progressive effects of the lay-off, it is desirable to follow a definite group of workers through a period of their unemployment.

The opportunity to do this is presented by the fact that the Institute of Human Relations is already in possession of the work and wage records of the former employes of the L. Candee and Company for eleven months following the lay-off in April, 1929. A re-survey of these individuals in 1932 makes possible a description of a three-year period of readjustment. The story of the last two years is not, strictly speaking, a history of readjustment. It is the history of the depression and its effects upon the lives of a normal group of workers, all of whom in comparatively prosperous times had fallen victim to the hazard of all workers, the lay-off.

Here is a group of workers who with very few exceptions had had regular employment for the twelve months preceding April, 1929. On April 6 the plant closed down. How successful was this group in making provision for self-maintenance, how close did they come to approximating the experience of their last full year of employment, 1928?

Number Seeking Work

In the reporting of this survey, every effort has been made to eliminate from consideration all who were not genuinely seeking work for the whole period. There is, of course, the possibility of error in judgment on the part of the interviewers. But the judgments were made not on the basis of the simple answer to a question, but on the basis of questioning as to methods used in the search for work, the answer to which could be interpreted in the light of the interviewer's knowledge of the possibilities of securing work in New Haven. If the slightest doubt arose, the questioned schedule was eliminated from the tabulation. The effect of this policy is, if anything, to weight the averages in favor of work rather than unemployment. But the results may be interpreted throughout as being true of those members of the group who for the whole three-year period were definitely in search of work.

A glance at Table 42 will indicate how the factors of increasing age and sex influenced the changing attitude toward self-support. Of the 8 men definitely not looking and presumably eligible for some type of work, 6 were above 45. Between the ages of 15 and 39 only 2 men were not seeking gainful employment.

The women had a much smaller proportion still in the labor market. Out of a total of 330, 101 had ceased looking for work. The bread winning role of the man stands out in this comparison. The possession of a family or a husband will permit a woman to withdraw from searching. The man cannot. Since the women are concentrated in the younger age groups, the effect of age is not so noticeable.

Only 158 (out of 193) men and 204 (out of 330) women will be considered as seeking work for wages. It must be remembered, however, that of the 35 men not so considered, 27 were either pensioned or had undertaken their own businesses. These classifications do not admit of comparison with the regular wage earners. They will be considered separately later. But it is clear that there is little indication at the end of three years that among the men the incentive to work had disappeared to any significant degree.

The accounts given the interviewers of the dreary and discouraging search for jobs which did not exist would build a graphic picture of the trip hammer blows under which this desire for work and wages has survived.

TIME UNEMPLOYED

The first significant indication of the effect of unemployment is that furnished by the number of months of working time lost in the years following the lay-off.

The men lost 35.5 per cent of the possible working time, the women 39.2 per cent in the first twelve months.[1] During the following year both men and women decreased the amount of unemployment, the men losing 33.2 per cent and the women 29.3 per cent of possible working time. The next year, however, found working time reduced beyond the amount secured in the first year, the per cent of time unemployed for men and women respectively being 40.2 and 31.3.[2]

The better employment record of the women is obvious after the first year when the industrial depression had begun to make itself felt. While the men were losing an average of 4.4 months a year, the women were losing 4.0 months. A part of this better record is explained, of course, by the fact that, in computing the averages, we have eliminated from consideration those women who definitely withdrew from the labor market. But it is also due to the fact that sewing trade labor was increasingly offering itself as alternative employment for women. (A discussion of

[1] Messrs. Clague and Couper found the lost time for the first eleven months equal to 36.9 per cent for the men and 41.7 per cent for the women. The wages of the twelve months following the lay-off were found by these investigators to be for men 53.6 per cent and for women 51.8 per cent of the 1928 income. Our figures on income are 58.7 per cent for men and 55.5 per cent for women. Several facts explain these differences. In the first place, we eliminated on the basis of the three years' record a number (largely women) who were obviously not looking for work. Although all of these had poor records up to the time of the first investigation, they could not be eliminated as "not looking" at that time. In the second place, all expectancy of help from the Institute had passed by the third year. Investigators were instructed to make no promises in the first investigation, but the hope was there in a number of cases. Such hope would tend to bias the informant in favor of a poorer work and wage record. We uncovered some jobs in the second investigation which had been omitted in the first. The net result is that our figures are somewhat weighted on the side of work and larger incomes.

[2] Table 43 in Appendix E, p. 144, and Chart V, p. 87.

this element in the employment history of women will be found later in this report).

The cases are too few to admit of any adequate determination of the importance of age in this employment experience. In general the age groups 30–44 among the men were most successful during the whole three-year period as the earlier survey found they had been during the first year. These groups lost an average of from 2.6 to 2.7 months a year while the average for the whole group was 4.4 months. The men over 50 continued to spend more than half of the year without work, an average of from 7.2 to 8.4 months[1] of unemployment being characteristic of these age groups.[2] There is not such a definite grouping of employment experience among the women according to age. The best record for the three years was made by the women 45–49 years of age. They lost an average of 2.2 months a year while the average for the whole group was 4.0 months. The younger women under 30 show less unemployment than any of the older age groups save this one, their average loss of time ranging from 3.1 to 3.7 months a year. It is useless, however, to attempt conclusions as to the age factor when several of the groups contain so few individuals.

The facts stand out, however, that in none of the three years did the men work more than 67 per cent of the time nor the women more than 71 per cent of the time, and that the women who remained in the labor market were, on the whole, more successful than the men in locating work. In spite of the increasing decline in industrial activity in 1930–31 the workers continued their readjustment with a slightly better record than the first year. But the fact that 33.2 per cent and 40.2 per cent of the men's time during the second and third twelve-month periods, respectively, was spent without work would indicate that the effect of the lay-off was by no means represented by an initial period of unemployment followed by a "steady job." In the case of these workers the readjustment of the first year was far from permanent.

[1] The one man in the 65–69 group who had only 1.7 months out of work is obviously an exception to the rule.
[2] Table 44 in Appendix E, p. 145.

CHART V

TIME UNEMPLOYED 1929–1932

(Expressed in percentages of total time. The twelve-month period extends from April to April)

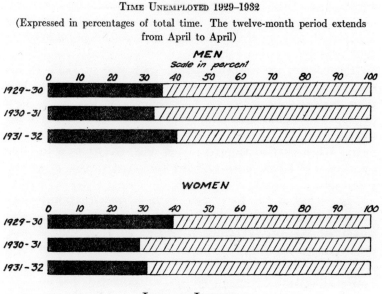

MEN
Scale in percent

WOMEN

LOSS OF INCOME

Another and more accurate way of measuring the change in economic status of the workers is to observe the size of their incomes for the period under discussion. The actual company figures for 1928 (their last full year of employment) were used as a base line. In the first twelve-month period the men earned 58.7 per cent, the women 55.5 per cent of the 1928 income. The women bettered this average in the following year, their income rising to 59.5 per cent of the 1928 income; but it fell back to 50.6 per cent during the third twelve months. The men's earnings declined steadily to a level of 54.2 per cent of the 1928 income during the second year after the lay-off, and to 44.6 per cent during the third year.[1]

Among the men the superior employment records of the 30–44 age groups (the three-year average ranging from 53.8 per cent in the 40–44 group to 66.3 per cent in the 30–34 group) are mirrored in their superior income records. The men over 50 (with

[1] Table 45 in Appendix E, p. 145, and Chart VI, p. 89.

the one exception in the 65–69 age group) retained on the average over the three-year period only from 27.3 to 32.7 per cent of their 1928 earning power. During these three years the average annual earnings of the whole group were 52.5 per cent of the 1928 earnings.[1]

Reference to the average earnings indicated in Table 46 will disclose the experience of the older men. As long as they held their regular jobs with the L. Candee and Company, their employability and effectiveness as workers (as indicated by wages) were equal to and possibly superior to that of the younger men. When they attempted to sell that effectiveness to other purchasers of labor, however, their comparative lack of success is obvious.

The record of the 15–19 age group is somewhat surprising. That they should earn annually more than their 1928 income would not have been expected in view of the average experience, even after considering that many of them became eligible for a man's wages during this time.

The situation is summarized by the statement that an average wage in 1928 for the men of $1,250.41 and for the women of $761.89 declined steadily in each of the three years until in the third year the average man was receiving $557.00 and the average women $385.73.

Factor of Skill

Two factors, sex and age, which have affected the employment history of this group of workers have been noted. A further factor may be considered: the degree of skill which the workers had attained prior to the lay-off. Presumably ability and initiative had received their reward on the job by increasing status and wages. Such at least is our common assumption. Did the same ability and initiative responsible for such advance *on the job* yield equally desirable results in efforts to get a job? The experience of the group is instructive on this point.

First, consider the records of the 158 men.[2] During the entire period the semi-skilled men fared best when extent of time un-

---

[1] Table 46 in Appendix E, p. 146.
[2] Table 47 in Appendix E, p. 146, Chart VII, p. 90 and Chart VIII, p. 91.

CHART VI

ANNUAL EARNINGS 1929–1932

(Expressed in percentages of 1928 earnings. The twelve-month period
extends from April to April)

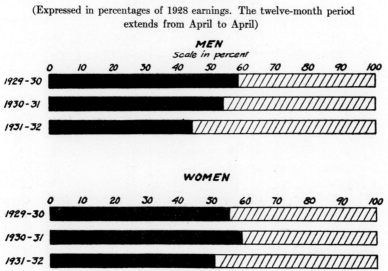

employed is considered; the skilled men fared worst. The per
cent of time unemployed for each of the three years was for the
semi-skilled 31.3, 30.4, and 37.7, respectively. For the unskilled,
the comparable percentages were 37.6, 33.5, and 40.3. For the
skilled the comparable percentages were 39.9, 36.9, and 43.9.

One would naturally expect that the decline in income would
be greater for the skilled group. It would have the most to
lose. While the skilled men were getting in each of the three
years 50.0 per cent, 50.8 per cent, and 36.2 per cent respectively
of their 1928 incomes, the semi-skilled were getting 63.6 per cent,
54.2 per cent, and 47.4 per cent, and the unskilled were getting
62.3 per cent, 59.7 per cent, and 51.7 per cent.

This comparatively good record of the unskilled is in part due
of course to the fact that its 1928 wages are lower than those of
the other groups. Only during the last year did the absolute
amount for laborers surpass that of the skilled. In that year
the average wage was $539.30 for the former and $505.34 for the
latter. The semi-skilled during the first and third years had the

CHART VII

UNEMPLOYMENT OF THE THREE SKILL GROUPS IN EACH OF THREE YEARS FOLLOWING SHUTDOWN

(Expressed in percentages of full time. The twelve-month period extends from April to April.

Degree of skill represents status as L. Candee worker)

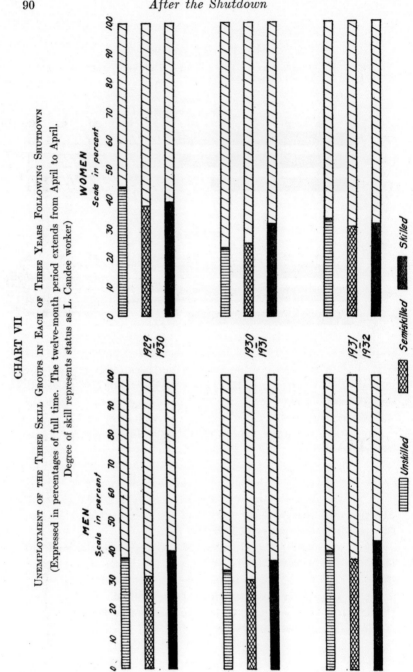

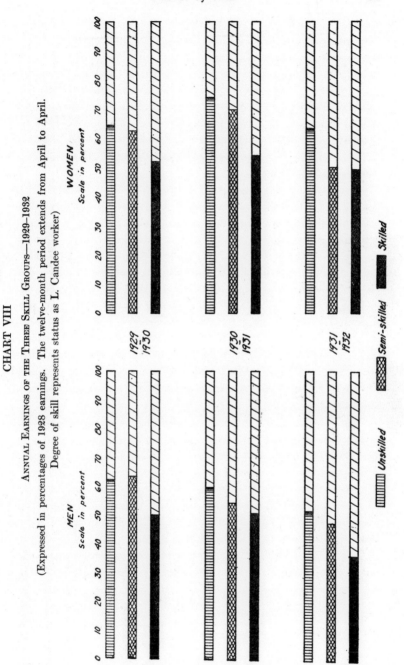

CHART VIII

ANNUAL EARNINGS OF THE THREE SKILL GROUPS—1929–1932

(Expressed in percentages of 1928 earnings. The twelve-month period extends from April to April.
Degree of skill represents status as L. Candee worker)

largest absolute wage, in these years surpassing the average of the skilled men by about $100. During the first year of readjustment, the average skilled man made only $46 more than the unskilled. During the last year the latter actually surpassed him by $34. Compare this with the advantage of $124 over the semi-skilled and $352 over the unskilled which the average skilled man had in 1928. If the standard of living in 1928 was proportionate to the amount of wage, the shock to the standard of living involved in readjustment was obviously the most severe for the skilled group.

The interpretation suggested by these facts is that the skilled man has been continuously forced to resort to jobs requiring less and less skill and paying lower wages. It is not possible to tell unerringly from a worker's description of his last job the degree of skill involved. Nevertheless it has been possible to make a rough estimate from those descriptions and there is least chance of error in the conclusions regarding unskilled labor.

Of the 48 skilled men who left the L. Candee and Company, 8 retained their status, 8 took semi-skilled jobs, and 32 were doing the work of laborers. Twelve of the 70 semi-skilled men did not alter their status, 8 advanced to skilled work, but 50 of them resorted to unskilled jobs. The unskilled laborer could, of course, fall into no lesser category; indeed, 9 of the 40 increased their status.[1]

The loss in status involved is equally obvious if the whole group is considered. Whereas the distribution on April 6, 1929, was 30.4 per cent, 44.3 per cent, and 25.3 per cent for skilled, semi-skilled, and unskilled jobs, respectively, the comparative distribution on April 1, 1932 was 11.4 per cent, 17.1 per cent, and 71.5 per cent, a change which involved 62 per cent and 61 per cent decreases in the skilled and unskilled classifications and a gain of 183 per cent in the unskilled group.[2]

The situation with the women is not so clear cut except when the decrease in income from the 1928 level is considered.[3] Here

[1] Table 49 in Appendix E, p. 147.
[2] Table 50 in Appendix E, p. 148, and Chart IX, p. 93.
[3] Table 48 in Appendix E, p. 147.

CHART IX

CHANGE IN JOB STATUS

(Per cent of all workers classified as skilled, semi-skilled, and unskilled on L. Candee job and on last job)

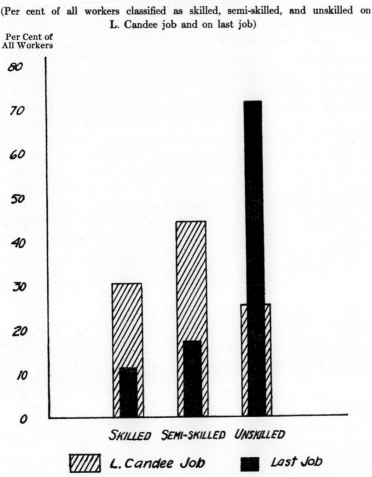

Per Cent of
All Workers

SKILLED   SEMI-SKILLED   UNSKILLED

▨ L. Candee Job   ■ Last Job

the per cent of 1928 income attained during each of the three years following the lay-off is: for the skilled, 52.1, 54.2 and 49.3; for the semi-skilled, 62.2, 69.9 and 50.1; for the unskilled, 64.6, 74.1 and 63.5. As in the case of the men the skilled group suffered most, the unskilled least in declining earning power.

Here is surely one of the most tragic results of unemployment. The men with the highest status as measured by their attainments on the job have the least success in maintaining their standard of living when the lay-off comes. Our ideas of reward for merit among workmen are premised on the idea that there are jobs in which that merit may exert itself and be rewarded. But this latter condition is necessary to the validity of our ideas. The task a man faces when the job goes may call for different qualities from those called for by steady employment. Apparently the very specialization and application to the learning of a valuable skill make a man less fitted than his workmate of lower occupational status for the task of readjustment. There is food for thought here, if such an experience were to prove typical of that of other American workers. We have assumed that there is a rough correlation between ability and the rewards of ability. Have we left out of account the fact that the spells of unemployment are as normal an occurrence as (somewhat longer) periods of work for a great many workmen?

The interviews with these formerly skilled men disclose another important result. The very keenness and initiative which among other things had made these men comparatively more valuable on the job bring them more quickly to a state of discouragement and despair, as status is lost. This is not the place to discuss the satisfactions which motivate and stimulate workers. But it is worth noting that the memory of a former achievement, now lost and apparently beyond recovery, is a goad whose prongs strike more forcefully the higher that occupational achievement has been. The effects of unemployment are in no case more cutting than in the case of the formerly skilled worker who has been forced to "take anything."

Loss in Purchasing Power

We have been considering the effect on the incomes of the workers as an individual problem. The adjustment made necessary for the workers is severe, the adjustment which the community faces is just as severe. The loss in purchasing power, the increasing numbers who are detached from the normal expenditure of time in productive work, the increasing relief burden, all of these represent a burden of provision for maintenance which has been transferred from industry to the community.

Consider the decrease in the amount of purchasing power available from wages.[1] During 1928 these workers then employed with the L. Candee and Company received in wages a total of $352,989.06. During each of the three years following the lay-off, the income of identically the same group from wages was $202,452.36, $199,564.42, and $166,693.34, respectively. Putting it differently, this group had from wage income $150,536.70 less to spend in the first twelve months after the lay-off than in the full year of 1928. This decrease grew to $153,424.64 in the second twelve months and mounted to $186,294.72 in the third twelve months.

This does not, of course, represent the true decline in purchasing power since the community subsidized many of these families through relief work, and public and private outright relief. Furthermore the United States Rubber Company paid terminal wages amounting to $35,440 to 69 members of the group we are considering. This amount was practically all expended during the first twelve months. The Company also paid in each of the three years in pensions to 35 individuals in the group, $12,375, $12,638, and $12,426, respectively. These pensioners on their own account added earnings for each of the three years of $2,444, $2,500, and $2,236. The actual yearly income (including all these sources) of the group as compared with the 1928 figure of $352,989 is for each of the successive twelve-month periods following the lay-off, $252,711, $214,702, and $181,356. Table 54-C in Appendix E gives figures on the extent to which public and private relief made up the resulting deficit. It would not be correct to draw conclusions from these figures without considering that wage scales had declined in New Haven between 1928 and 1932.

Nevertheless, the cold fact remains that the income of this group, derived from the wages of workers, produced in the third year after the lay-off $186,294.72 less than the $352,989.06 produced from this source in 1928. Workers cannot spend money they do not receive.

[1] Tables 51-A and 51-B in Appendix E, p. 148.

MEASUREMENT OF THE UNEMPLOYMENT PROBLEM

One of the interesting possibilities in a study of this kind is the testing of the validity of the employment or unemployment average as a true measure of the problem created by unemployment. From the point of view of social administration, the problem of unemployment is represented by its cumulative effect. A thousand men who have been out of work for one week are less of a social problem than a hundred men who have been out of work for ten weeks. The depleted incomes, the growth of anti-social attitudes, ill effects on health, initiative, and industrial efficiency are correlated not so much with numbers out of work on any particular date as with the length of time during which they have had no jobs. It is the adding of week after week to the period in which one has no place in a working world which undermines a man's ability to support himself, decreases his confidence in his capacity for that task, and produces the lines outside the doors of public and private charity agencies. It is the length of time since the lay-off which determines for families and other institutions in the community the severity of the problem of finding satisfactory alternatives for the expenditure of time which formerly was occupied in useful production.

Consider two ways of representing unemployment with these facts in mind. If we consider the per cent in the group who were unemployed at the beginning of each month from April, 1929, to April, 1932, the figures show considerable variation.[1] From a high point of 69 per cent on April 6, 1929, the percentage of men unemployed decreases fairly regularly to a low point of 26 per cent on January 1, 1930. Nine months after the shutdown the maximum number had found jobs. From this point on, the number unemployed started to increase. The adjustments made and the new jobs obtained during the first nine months did not prove permanent for many. Between March and December, 1930, the per cent unemployed hovers between 31 and 34, seasonal variations being somewhat lost in the general slowing down of industrial activity. During the year 1931 the figure

[1] Table 52 in Appendix E, p. 149.

again rises from 36.7 per cent unemployed in January to 43.7 per cent in December. By the end of the survey period in April, 1932, nearly half of the men were again out of work. The record of the women shows a somewhat narrower range of fluctuation. After the initial and slightly irregular decrease in unemployment from a high point of 70.6 per cent on April 6, 1929, to a low point of 26.5 per cent in November, 1930, (almost identical with the men's low point) the percentages kept within the five-point range of between 28.4 and 33.3 to the termination of the survey period.

The picture presented by such a measurement is that the employment situation of the men grew steadily better for nine months and then climbed over a series of plateaus back toward the situation at the lay-off. Among the women the employment situation grew better, with a few irregular months, for 19 months, then varied little for the rest of the period.

Now turn to the other method of recording the severity of unemployment. The cumulative effects of unemployment may be represented by the number of months of unemployment which had accumulated for the workers on the first of each month. For convenience this has been recorded in Table 53 as number of months unemployed for the average worker. Starting with .4 of a month for the men on May 1, 1929, the increase of time unemployed is a steady one. At no time does the rise become less pronounced. The same thing is true of the women. It is interesting to note that the records of the men and the women varied only slightly, although by the end of the thirty-sixth month, the men had had on the average 13.1 months of unemployment and the women 11.9 months, a difference of approximately a month.

The accumulated amount of time without a job increased without much relationship to the numbers unemployed at any particular time. And in that increase is grounded a cumulative problem for the community and its agencies, for the families of these workers, and for the workers themselves. The story of what unemployment does, the record of the intensity of its burden, is represented most accurately in such a picture.

CHART X

Extent of Unemployment over Three-Year Period, April, 1929, to April, 1932: Months Unemployed by Average Worker Compared with Per Cent Unemployed (Men)

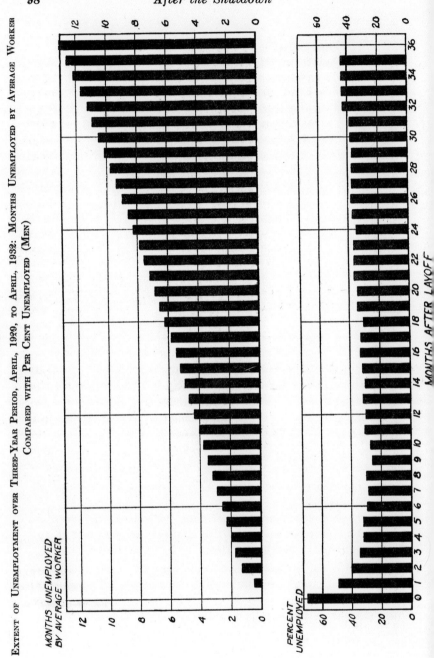

CHART XI

EXTENT OF UNEMPLOYMENT OVER THREE-YEAR PERIOD, APRIL, 1929, TO APRIL, 1932: MONTHS UNEMPLOYED BY AVERAGE WORKER COMPARED WITH PER CENT UNEMPLOYED (WOMEN)

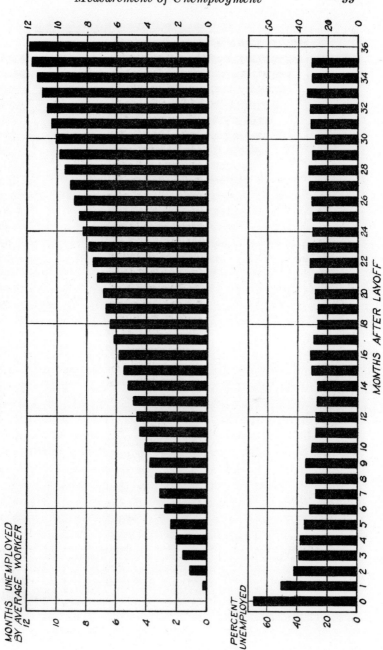

PUBLIC AND PRIVATE RELIEF

When the normal source of self support is curtailed, when industry ceases to supply wages or sufficient wages, the worker is forced to resort to other means. The lay-off of April, 1929, coming at the beginning of a period of industrial stagnation, did not, however, suddenly introduce this group of workers to public and private charity. Fifty-one families had already made the acquaintance of relief agencies before the lay-off.[1] Their experience with the agencies is represented in Chart XII.[2] The war-time boom, the after-war prosperity, and the alternate periods of " hard " and " good " times in the Coolidge prosperity era are plainly written in the fluctuations there recorded. The L. Candee workers were not an unusual group and furnished representatives throughout the period to the case load of the agencies.

During the first twelve months after the lay-off only nine new families resorted to charity. But the next two years witnessed increases of 44 and 47 families respectively. During the thirty-six months after the plant shut down, the number of families receiving help from public and private charity grew nearly 200 per cent.

The increasing load on the community is obvious from the amounts expended on members of this group by relief agencies.[3] When the absolute figures are read, the increasing of the relief expenditures from $3,412 to $4,471 to $13,328 seems a considerable burden on taxes and public generosity. But Chart XIII will indicate how little of the burden of unemployment the community actually carried, how predominately the loss in wage income was carried by the workers themselves and to a lesser degree by their former employer. If we consider their income for 1928 as 100 per cent, we find 99.9 per cent of it furnished by wages, 0.1 per cent by charity. Now follow the group through

[1] Table 54-A in Appendix E, p. 150.
[2] Table 54-D in Appendix E, p. 152.
[3] The proportions borne by the public and private agencies as indicated by Table 54-C vary somewhat from those reported by the Governor's Unemployment Commission for the same period. With such a small group, the relief of one family in 1929 to the extent of $1,160 when the total public aid was $3,061 of course makes the public portion appear large. If the amount of public aid were corrected for this item, the trend toward the growing dominance of public relief would be obvious.

CHART XII

TOTAL AMOUNTS EXPENDED ON RELIEF TO L. CANDEE FAMILIES BY ALL
AGENCIES, 1913 TO 1932

(The shutdown occurred April 6, 1929. April 6 has therefore been used as
the beginning of each twelve-month period)

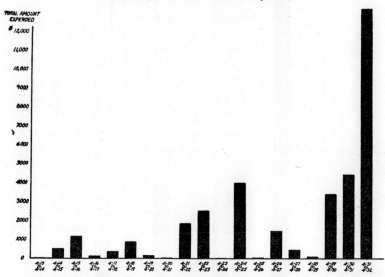

three twelve-month periods following the lay-off. In the first
period a decline in income of 42 per cent is offset by charity
amounting to 1 per cent of their 1928 income, and pensions
and terminal wages from the United States Rubber Company
amounting to 13.5 per cent of that 1928 figure. The workers
were faced with the problem of borrowing, selling, or curtailing
expenditures to adjust to the residue of the deficit amounting
to 27.5 per cent of their 1928 income. In the next period while
charity increased to 1.3 per cent, the terminal wage boon had
passed,[1] leaving only pensions coming from the Company. The
result found the workers with a net deficit of 37.7 per cent of
their 1928 income. The next year, in spite of the increasing
amount from charity, the workers, their wage incomes decreas-

[1] Clague and Couper's investigation disclosed that approximately four-fifths of the
amount from terminal wages had been spent within the first eleven months.

CHART XIII

PROPORTION OF INCOME FROM SEVERAL SOURCES FOR 1928 AND FOR THREE ONE-YEAR PERIODS, 1929–1932

[Note: (1) includes $2,444 in wages of pensioners; (2) includes $2,500 in wages of pensioners; (3) includes $2,236 in wages of pensioners]

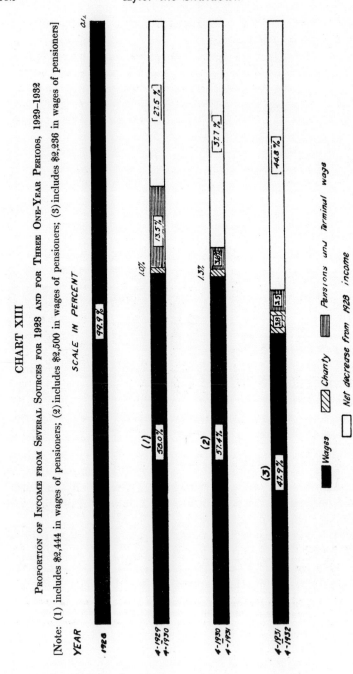

YEAR

SCALE IN PERCENT

1928　　99.9%　　0.1%

(1)　　53.0%　　1.0%　　13.5%　　[27.5 %]
4-1929
4-1930

(2)　　57.4%　　1.3%　　5.5%　　[37.7 %]
4-1930
4-1931

(3)　　47.9%　　5.8　　3.5　　[44.8 %]
4-1931
4-1932

■ Wages　　▨ Charity　　▥ Pensions and Terminal wages　　□ Net decrease from 1928 income

ing, had to readjust their standard of living to a decrease of 44.8 per cent of their 1928 income.

Putting the matter differently, the curtailing of wages left in each year a growing burden, which may be represented as the difference between the wage income of 1928 and the wage income of each succeeding twelve-month period following the lay-off. In the first year the approximate proportions of this burden borne by the three sources were:

Charity	2.4 per cent
Company	32.1 per cent
Workers	65.5 per cent

during the second year:

Charity	3.1 per cent
Company	8.4 per cent
Workers	88.5 per cent

during the third year:

Charity	7.3 per cent
Company	6.7 per cent
Workers	86.0 per cent

In spite of the efforts of the community to bear the burden of unemployment through private contributions and taxes, the real "burden of unemployment" still rests upon the shoulders of the unemployed themselves. It is they who sustain the major shock, drastically curtail their expenditures, and readjust their standard of living in the face of the failure of the community's job supply. Whatever may be true of specific individuals, the workers as a group are not unloading their burden upon the community.[1]

PENSIONED WORKERS

A number of the workers were given pensions ranging from the minimum of $20 a month to a maximum of $106.55. Of

---

[1] An incidental finding coming from this material is the extent to which there was a sharing by various agencies of the responsibility for the relief of specific families. A glance at Table 54-B will indicate what proportions of the cases were cared for by one agency alone. The Department of Public Charities shared responsibility for the care of over twice as many as it cared for alone; the Citizen's Committee on Employment (relief work) cared for about an equal number by itself and in co-operation with other agencies; Private Agency No. 1, helping five families alone, assisted nearly nine times as many who received other aid. Private Agency No. 2 gave supplementary relief to over seven times as many as it carried alone. The first adjustment to this situation was made in October, 1932, by a re-allocation of cases, a process which was completed by March, 1933.

this group, 14 men and 21 women were interviewed in 1932. If their pension is included in their income, how had they fared in comparison with the others?

The average earnings for all seeking work for the three years following the shutdown were:

	'29–'30	'30–'31	'31–'32
Women	$423.52	$453.09	$385.73
Men	734.52	678.07	557.00

If to the pensions received are added the earnings of two women and four men who worked for income in addition to their pensions, we find the average annual income of the pensioned group for the three years to be as follows:

	'29–'30	'30–'31	'31–'32
Women	$347.06	$340.66	$333.67
Men	537.98	570.33	546.93

The wages which the workers who were in the active industrial field were able to get fell very close to the income level of those who were pensioned, particularly during the last year.

The part which pensions alone played in this total may be seen from the following average yearly pensions for the 3 twelve month periods:

	'29–'30	'30–'31	'31–'32
Women	$287.87	$294.00	$289.10
Men	452.14	461.76	454.08

How far had these pensions succeeded in keeping the families concerned from the necessity of going to the relief agencies? Three of the workers resorted to the funds of public or private charity during the period under survey. Two of these were women. Each had one small requisition from the Department of Public Charities. The man, a negro, had one week's work from the Citizen's Committee on Employment.

This record is testimony either to the adequacy of the pensions to meet the needs of the pensioners, or the ability of the workers to trim their needs to suit their resources.

INDEPENDENT BUSINESS

" Why don't you set up for yourself? " is a question frequently put to a man who loses his job as a wage earner. Thirteen men and 4 women out of the 523 individuals reporting tried this method of self support. The conditions of their choice and their experiences are interesting.

The first problem facing the worker who wishes to "set up" for himself is the need for capital. The fact that L. Candee and Company provided a terminal wage for some of its employes provided 8, or nearly half of the 17, with a source of funds. Two of these saved the amount for periods after the shutdown of twenty-three and thirty months respectively before investing it in a business. The others invested soon after the lay-off. Four obtained their capital from savings and 4 from loans advanced by relatives. One turned to a small loan company. The possession of the terminal wage was an important factor in suggesting independent business as an alternative.

The choice of business is somewhat limited by the amount of capital available. The largest group, 6, started grocery or meat stores. Only 4 entered the trade, shoe repairing, which might appear logical for workers whose occupation was closely allied to that trade. Candy and cigars, and pool rooms attracted in each case the investments of 2 individuals. One of these operated a speakeasy in connection with his candy shop. Hat cleaning, fruit peddling, a gas station, and a rooming house each was tried by one worker.

Age and skill seem to have a relationship to the suggestion that independent business can be the solution of one's maintenance problems. All but 2 of the men were over 40. With the exception of one man of 28 years and one of 32 years, such an alternative did not appeal to the younger men. The fact that increased age carried with it savings, credit, and the right to terminal wage is probably more important here than the factor of age. The same statement could be made regarding the factor of skill. Only one unskilled man undertook to manage a business. Three of the women were skilled and one semi-skilled. Eight and 4 men were in these two classes respectively.

Over half of the group, 9, started within three months; 11 had started before six, and 13 before twelve months had elapsed. The remaining 4 did not begin until two years after the lay-off.

How well did they succeed—these workers who tried breaking

new paths? Our survey did not ask for balance sheets; indeed, the accounting systems of such small concerns, some of them kept on the backs of paper bags, could not have furnished such an item. But the conversations with these workers disclosed their estimate of their own achievements. Only 5 of the group were making money, 8 were discouraged and declared they were running behind or barely making expenses. Five had failed, losing amounts ranging from $300 to $600.

Such a record is not surprising when one considers that only 2 had had any previous training whatever in independent endeavor and only 1 of these had had experience in the specific business he set up.

The outlook of this group of workers is definitely that of a wage earner. When they survey the possibilities before them their imagination seldom, and their experience still more seldom, places before them the choice of setting up for themselves. The measure of success achieved by this small group would not serve as a very active incentive to unemployed workers, in the districts where these people live, to get out of the wage earning class. Such facts as these help to build the walls which hold men and women in the occupational class into which they were born.

Sewing Trades

During the period of time for which the employment records of the workers were studied, considerable agitation arose concerning the invasion of New Haven by a number of needlework shops, commonly called "sweat shops." The subject of the regulation of these concerns has been the focus of a good deal of welfare, industrial, and political activity. Much of this has been undertaken in an atmosphere highly charged with emotional reactions. It is hard under such circumstances to get at the facts. The Women's Bureau of the United States Department of Labor has undertaken a thorough investigation of this matter, however, which is providing the basis for minimum wage legislation.

The contribution of our survey to the subject is not extensive. It consists of several data which came to light incidentally in the course of charting the work and wage records of the women who worked formerly for the L. Candee and Company. One of the obvious alternatives to which women workers might turn was the sewing trade. How much of their re-employment was accounted for by such work, what did they get in wages, and how strong was the suggestion made by the presence of these shops in the immediate neighborhood?

The proportion of all employment represented by sewing trades increased steadily over the three-year period. From close to ¼ during the first twelve months following the lay-off, it rose to approximately ⅓ during the second period, and to about ⅖ during the last twelve months.[1]

During the second twelve months this type of labor represented a real increase in jobs. During the third period the gain is more than counteracted by the loss in other jobs. The interesting fact here is that recourse to the sewing trades increases as economic recession becomes more intense.

CHART XIV

DISTRIBUTION OF EMPLOYMENT BETWEEN SEWING TRADES AND OTHER JOBS, 1929–1932 (WOMEN)

(The twelve-month period extends from April to April)

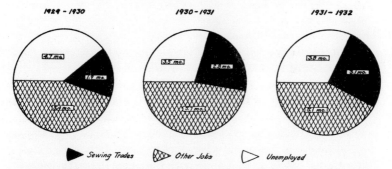

If the age groups are considered, it is seen that the youngest, 15–19 years, lost most heavily in regular industrial employment, but saved themselves from correspondingly severe unemployment by recourse to sewing trade labor to a greater degree than any other group. In general the sewing trade adjustment is more characteristic of women under 34 than of those over that

[1] Table 55, p. 152, and Table 56, p. 153, in Appendix E, and Chart XIV.

age. In the three lower age groups, i. e., below 30, this is matched by a higher employment record in other jobs as well.

The wages which this group received for their work do not indicate such a low wage scale as that commonly attributed to this industry.[1] In general they average from two to three dollars less a week than those received by individuals of the same group in other employment. Sewing trade weekly wages decreased in each successive year as did other wages. The decrease in the former is pictured in the weekly average for each of the three years respectively of $11.14, $10.63, and $9.60. The corresponding weekly rates in other wages were $14.17, $13.15, $11.53. There is a difference here between sewing trade rates and other rates of $3.03, $2.52, and $1.93 a week in each successive year.[2]

The age groups which show appreciable variation from the average are influenced by one important factor among others, that supervisors have been drawn from these groups. The increase in wages from $8.70 in the first to $11.55 in the second twelve months in the 25–29 year age group is a direct result of this fact. The numbers in the 30–34 age group were small and the wage level of $14.08 is directly related to the number of supervisors in this group. It should be pointed out that members of this group had the highest wage level of any of the groups when they found work in other occupations.

There is one section of New Haven which has a particularly large number of sewing trade establishments. Wards 10, 11, and 12 (which incidentally are the wards containing the largest percentage of Italians in the city) are sometimes called "the sweat shop district." The presence of the establishments in the immediate neighborhood evidently played a large part in suggesting the possibility of such work during the first two years after the lay-off.[3] During the first year the workers in the three wards mentioned had a definitely better employment record than the others. But this better record corresponded almost exactly to the difference in amounts of sewing labor performed by the two

---

[1] Table 57 in Appendix E, p. 153.

[2] The Women's Bureau of the U. S. Department of Labor found the median wage of 7,631 women in Connecticut Sewing Trade establishments to be even higher than this ($12.35) in the fall of 1931. *Employment of Women in the Sewing Trades of Connecticut, Bulletin No. 97*, Women's Bureau of the U. S. Department of Labor, p. 6.

[3] Table 58 in Appendix E, p. 153.

groups. The same fact is true of the second year with the exception that a difference of .7 of a month in the amount of other employment was partially made up in sewing labor by the smaller group. During the third year the group in wards 10, 11, and 12 lost heavily in other employments, but still, due to their sewing trade labor, had over a half a month less unemployment than the others.

There is no evidence that these women in wards 10, 11, and 12 were more proficient in needlework than the others. That they turned to a larger degree to such work is one indication of the respective parts played by ability and by chance opportunity in determining the direction in which the worker turns for a chance for employment.

The sewing trades thrive on a depression in industrial activity. Worker after worker in these trades declared that her earnings would be unnecessary and would cease if her husband, or father, or brother could secure a job. We found very few who did not declare that they would quit the sewing trades if it were not the only thing one could find to do.

"Just let the L. Candee, or any big factory for that matter, get going, and see how quick I'd leave that shirt place" is the statement of one which may serve for practically all. The so-called "sweat shop" comes into the neighborhood offering employment when other firms have dismissed their workers and left them without work. The turning to such work is as characteristic of the women's adjustment as the turning to casual labor is of that of the men. It is in part the result of the efforts of these workers to support themselves. It is the realistic adjustment involved for them when they display the kind of initiative I have heard individuals attribute to themselves when they say, "If I were out of work, I'd take anything before I'd go to charity."

It will be fortunate if the minimum wage legislation now being urged in Connecticut does become effective at the moment when industrial activities generally are increasing. The attitudes of the sewing trade workers indicate that if such concerns are to keep operating in such a period, their wage scale will have to rise considerably in order to attract workers whose male relatives are back at work and who themselves could find jobs in the other industries and businesses of the community. The administration of the law will be reinforced by the normal demands of competition for labor.

SUMMARY

We may quickly call attention to the most prominent features of the picture of a three-year adjustment to unemployment.

(1) The experience had not cancelled noticeably the search for work in the case of the men in spite of the impact of the discouraging search for jobs that didn't exist. Many of the women, though presumably still eligible, had definitely withdrawn from the labor market, a fact not surprising in view of the normal economic dependency of wives and mothers.

In none of the three years following the lay-off on April 6, 1929, did the average man work more than 67 per cent of the time, nor the average woman more than 71 per cent. The decline in working time and wages was steady. The readjustment during the first eleven months pictured in Part I of this report was not to steady work, but to a set of jobs which produced a decreasing amount of work and wages in each succeeding year. The particularly unfavorable position of the older men is obvious and the best records were made by the age groups from 30–44 years.

The fact that on April 6, 1929, this entire group had a high degree of employability in its own trade (as evidenced by the fact that they actually were holding jobs) would indicate that the reason for loss of time did not lie in unemployability. That employable workers can, in three years after a lay-off, secure work on the average only two-thirds of the time and earn little more than half of their former full time wages is an indication of the forces back of unemployment outside of the workers' control. The decline in average earnings from the 1928 figure of $1250.41 for the men and $761.89 for the women to $557.00 and $385.73 respectively during the third year after the lay-off represents the gulf which the workers must have bridged if they were to maintain their standard of living. The feat was obviously impossible.

(2) The skilled man on the whole suffered most from the readjust-

ment in regard to time out of work, decline in wages, and actual earnings. By the third year his average annual earnings were $34 less than those of the unskilled and $98 less than those of the semi-skilled man. The shock to the standard of living is greatest in his case. More than that, it has resulted in a loss of job status which is well pictured in the fact that the last jobs were reported as skilled in only 11 per cent of the cases compared with 30 per cent in the L. Candee employment. The proportions of unskilled jobs on the other hand had risen from 25 per cent in the L. Candee employment to 71 per cent in the last jobs. Apparently the qualities which help men to rise to skilled jobs and high wages *while at work* are of limited use in helping men to readjust satisfactorily *when the job goes*. That readjustment means in most cases a one way journey to work of less skill and lower wages with its consequent blow to the worker's standard of living and status, a blow most severe for the skilled who have most to lose.

The pensions distributed by the United States Rubber Company coupled with the management on the part of the pensioners succeeded in keeping all but three of the recipients off the rolls of public or private charity.

Independent business was an alternative which appealed to few, normally the older and skilled workers, and in half of the cases, to those who received a terminal wage which could be used as working capital. The small businesses which they set up or purchased were not operating successfully; five out of the seventeen had failed. Such a situation is not surprising in view of their lack of training. The possibilities revealed would not encourage many workers to abandon wage earning as a field for self support.

The sewing trades, paying from $2.00 to $3.00 less per week than other employment, accounted for from a quarter to two-fifths of all the jobs secured by women in each of the three years after April 6, 1929, the proportion growing as the depression increased in intensity. The younger women particularly were attracted to this alternative. The presence of the establishments in the neighborhood evidently suggested strongly the possibility of such employment, the heaviest recruiting being from neighborhoods immediately surrounding them. The dislike for such work was clearly apparent and indicated that minimum wage legislation would be materially easier to enforce when a period of rising wages and opening jobs forced sewing trade employers to balance a lack of attractiveness in the work itself with favorable wages.

The whole community felt the loss of jobs and wages involved in the lay-off. The accumulating burden of unemployment, which left the average worker at the end of three years with over a third of the period to spend in idleness, has community-wide effects. Many of them, such as the growth of anti-social attitudes, ill effects on health, on initiative, and on industrial efficiency, influences on family and institutional life are intangible as far as precise description is concerned. One result, however, is clear. The wages of this group gave them $186,294 less to spend in the third year after the lay-off than the $352,989 which they had to spend from that source in 1928.

Into the gap caused by lack of wages the United States Rubber Company and the community poured terminal wages, pensions and charity. But the gap was far from closed. If the difference between the 1928 income and wage income in each of the three years following the lay-off is taken as a measure of the burden of unemployment, the fact stands out that the three years found the workers themselves bearing 65 per cent, 88 per cent, and 86 per cent of that burden respectively. In spite of the efforts of the Company and the community, it is still the worker himself who must drastically revise his standard of living, search for alternative methods of maintenance when he faces unemployment, and through such efforts shoulder most of the load. In spite of mounting relief funds, unemployment is still predominately the workers' problem.

APPENDICES A, B, C, D
PART I

APPENDIX A

ANNUAL INCOME AND FAMILY INCOME IN RELATION TO WAGE RATES

Few statistical problems are so fraught with pitfalls as the collection of statistics of wage rates and earnings, especially when the earnings are expressed on an annual basis.[1] Furthermore, individual earnings are often of much less significance than family earnings as an indicator of the standard of living. Both these points will have significance in this study because of the discrepancy which existed between wage rates and earnings, and because of the large number of family relationships existing among the workers. On the first point—the comparison of wage rates with the actual annual earnings of the individual worker— a statistical analysis was made for all workers for whom comparable data could be secured. Because most of these workers were on piece rates, weekly earnings rather than hourly wage rates have been used for the purpose of calculating the theoretical full time annual earnings.

The computation was made as follows. On a card for each worker the Company kept a record of the actual weekly earnings for the calendar year. We selected from each card a period of eight successive weeks of sustained good earnings. The average weekly payment of this period was then considered to be the worker's full time weekly earnings under reasonably normal conditions. This period was not necessarily the same time of the year for all workers, although at the New Haven plant the majority of cases fell in the months of May, June and July when the plant was operating on a normally full schedule. This average weekly wage payment was then converted into an annual figure through multiplication by forty-eight. Forty-eight, rather than fifty-two, was used because the rubber plants were usually shut down about four weeks each year. Another reason for preferring forty-eight weeks as the basis of computation for trans-

[1] See Frain, *Earnings in Certain Standard Machine-Tool Occupations in Philadelphia*. University of Pennsylvania Press.

lating weekly earnings into annual income is that this may be considered fairly representative of full time in most industries throughout the country, even in prosperous years.

Against this figure of theoretical full time annual earnings was placed the total earnings actually paid by the Company to the wage earner in 1928 (New Haven). In the case of the Hartford plant the period January to August, 1929, was used, the eight months then being stepped up to a full year for purposes of comparison with New Haven. The results of these computations for the workers, classified by age groups, are shown in the following table.

TABLE 30

Ratio of Actual to Full Time Annual Earnings, by Age Groups

Age Group (1)	Number of Workers (2)	Mean Actual Annual Earnings (3)	Mean Full-Time Annual Earnings (4)	Percentage Ratio of Actual to Full-Time Earnings (3) ÷ (4)
		NEW HAVEN—WOMEN		
Total	*328*	*830.63*	*1048.19*	*79.2*
15–19	50	718.83	922.98	77.0
20–24	75	832.70	1045.33	78.3
25–29	68	847.86	1068.45	77.3
30–34	32	836.52	1189.11	78.0
35–39	34	974.46	1153.48	81.9
40–44	32	866.15	1081.39	80.1
45–49	18	805.42	1016.93	79.2
50–54	13	798.53	918.42	86.9
55–59	5	740.38	872.16	84.9
60–64	1	702.17	855.84	82.0
		NEW HAVEN—MEN		
Total	*193*	*1346.16*	*1538.42*	*87.5*
15–19	14	755.87	970.87	77.9
20–24	15	1115.55	1329.34	83.9
25–29	18	1515.58	1735.89	87.3
30–34	21	1546.79	1734.71	89.0
35–39	20	1431.97	1644.86	87.1
40–44	29	1487.11	1638.79	90.7
45–49	32	1306.17	1488.99	87.7
50–54	19	1387.11	1580.51	87.8
54–59	16	1409.13	1590.54	88.6
60–64	8	1132.63	1326.66	85.4
65–69	1	1205.24	1382.40	87.2
		HARTFORD—MEN		
Total	*440*	*1593.16*	*1811.98*	*87.9*
15–19	6	1170.34	1303.50	89.8
20–24	12	1479.08	1685.92	97.7
25–29	58	1548.01	1771.83	87.4
30–34	76	1605.80	1853.29	86.6
35–39	98	1650.41	1864.60	88.5
40–44	82	1630.54	1865.52	87.5
45–49	49	1595.09	1817.49	87.8
50–54	26	1554.50	1736.23	89.5
55–59	14	1460.93	1615.28	90.5
60–64	13	1595.46	1796.00	88.8
65–69	6	1530.00	1622.83	94.3

This table shows that 328 women in the New Haven plant, for example, averaged $830.63 in actual annual earnings for the year 1928. (Workers who had been either hired or laid off during the year were definitely excluded from the computation; these figures apply to workers attached to the plant throughout the year.) These same women, on the basis of what seemed to be their normal weekly earnings, should have received an average of $1048.19. As shown in the final column, the women earned 79 per cent of their theoretical full-time earnings. For the men the ratio of actual to full-time earnings was approximately the same in both plants, about 88 per cent.

For both men and women there is some evidence of greater steadiness in the older age groups. This was much more pronounced in the New Haven plant than in Hartford.

These figures show that women lose considerably more time at work than do men. To some extent the shortage of actual earnings was due to lack of orders at the plant, but this was not a significant factor in explaining the differences between the men and women. Even if it were assumed that the entire loss of the men was due to lack of work, it is still evident that women lose more time for personal reasons, illness, child-bearing, and the necessity of taking care of the home. Marital status apparently made little difference in this matter, the unmarried women showing practically as many absences as the married. Classification of the married women according to the number of their children seemed likewise to reveal nothing.

To some extent these averages of ratios by wage groups tend to conceal the much greater loss in time of individual workers. In order to bring out this point more clearly Table 31 is presented, showing the workers classified according to the ratio of actual to full-time annual earnings.

Once more the serious losses in time suffered by the women become evident. Less than 2 per cent of the men in Hartford and only 4 per cent of those in New Haven fell below a ratio of 75, while many more than half of all men in both places had ratios falling between 85 and 95. The women were entirely different. Over 9 per cent of them had a ratio of less than 60, which means that their actual annual earnings were less than

After the Shutdown

TABLE 31

Number and Percentage of Workers Receiving Actual Annual Earnings of Specified Percentage Ratios to Full Time Earnings

PERCENTAGE RATIO OF ACTUAL TO FULL-TIME ANNUAL EARNINGS	NUMBER OF WORKERS			PERCENTAGES OF TOTAL		
	New Haven		Hartford Men	New Haven		Hartford Men
	Women	Men		Women	Men	
Total	328	193	440	100.0	100.0	100.0
Less than 60.........	30	4	1	9.2	2.1	.2
60–64.................	8	3	..	2.4	1.5	..
65–69.................	22	..	4	6.7	...	.9
70–74.................	28	..	3	8.5	...	.7
75–79.................	27	10	22	8.2	5.2	5.0
80–84.................	74	26	79	22.6	13.5	18.0
85–89.................	85	63	128	25.9	32.6	29.1
90–94.................	42	60	121	12.8	31.1	27.5
95–99.................	11	17	75	3.4	8.8	17.0
100.................	1	10	7	.3	5.2	1.6

three-fifths of what they could have earned on full time. Only about 16 per cent of the women achieved ratios of 90 or above.

The averages given in Table 30 likewise conceal the spread in earnings between different wage groups. Table 32 shows the workers classified according to their actual annual earnings.

This table brings to light certain additional points of interest. About one-fourth of the women earned more than $1000 per

TABLE 32

Workers Classified According to Actual Annual Earnings

ACTUAL ANNUAL EARNINGS	NUMBER OF WORKERS			PERCENTAGES OF TOTAL		
	New Haven		Hartford Men	New Haven		Hartford Men
	Women	Men		Women	Men	
All Classes.....	328	193	440	100.0	100.0	100.0
Less than $400..	14	1	..	4.3	.5	....
400–499.........	15	1	..	4.6	.5	....
500–599.........	24	1	..	7.3	.5	....
600–699.........	42	6	..	12.8	3.1	....
700–799.........	49	2	1	14.9	1.0	.2
800–899.........	50	10	1	15.3	5.2	.2
900–999.........	48	11	2	14.6	5.7	.5
1000–1099.......	44	15	2	13.4	7.8	.5
1100–1199.......	21	21	10	6.4	10.9	2.3
1200–1299.......	18	20	21	5.5	10.4	4.8
1300–1399.......	2	21	43	.6	10.9	9.8
1400–1499.......	1	16	81	.3	8.3	18.4
1500–1599.......	..	23	83	...	11.9	18.9
1600–1699.......	..	12	68	...	6.2	15.4
1700–1799.......	..	13	61	...	6.7	13.9
1800–1899.......	..	9	31	...	4.7	7.0
1900–1999.......	..	8	15	...	4.2	3.4
2000–2099.......	..	1	7	...	.5	1.6
2100–2199.......	..	..	1	...	...	1.8
2200–2299.......	..	..	1	...	...	.2
2300 and Over..	..	2	5	...	1.0	1.1

year, but no woman reached $1500. On the other hand, in the same plant, very few men earned less than $800 and nearly 30 per cent earned in excess of $1500. In Hartford there were more men above $2000 than there were below $1200.

The workers in the lower earnings classes are there partly because of low wages and partly because of short time. The latter influence predominates in this particular situation. In order to segregate the influence of low wages from short time in determining the classifications shown in Table 32 the following table is presented for comparative purposes.

TABLE 33

Workers Classified According to Theoretical Full Time Annual Earnings

THEORETICAL FULL TIME ANNUAL EARNINGS	NUMBER OF WORKERS			PERCENTAGES OF TOTAL		
	New Haven		Hartford Men	New Haven		Hartford Men
	Women	Men		Women	Men	
All Classes	*328*	*193*	*440*	*100.0*	*100.0*	*100.0*
Less than $400 .	..	..	..	...	...	...
400–499.........	2	..	..	0.6	...	...
500–599.........	4	1	..	1.2	0.5	...
600–699.........	7	2	..	2.1	1.0	...
700–799.........	31	2	..	9.5	1.0	...
800–899.........	47	1	..	14.3	0.5	...
900–999.........	37	7	..	11.3	3.6	...
1000–1099.......	60	10	2	18.3	5.2	0.5
1100–1199.......	59	11	5	18.0	5.7	1.1
1200–1299.......	43	24	7	13.1	12.4	1.6
1300–1399.......	22	16	8	6.7	8.3	1.8
1400–1499.......	12	27	21	3.7	14.0	4.8
1500–1599.......	3	14	51	0.9	7.3	11.6
1600–1699.......	1	13	52	0.3	6.7	11.8
1700–1799.......	..	14	73	...	7.3	16.6
1800–1899.......	..	11	57	...	5.7	13.0
1900–1999.......	..	11	60	...	5.7	13.6
2000–2099.......	..	14	55	...	7.3	12.5
2100–2199.......	..	7	20	...	3.6	4.5
2200–2299.......	..	5	13	...	2.6	3.0
2300 and Over..	..	3	16	...	1.6	3.6

This shows the classification of workers by theoretical full time annual earnings. Attention may be called to the data for the women. In this table there are none in the class less than $400 and only thirteen in the classes less than $700. Considerably more than one-third of the women now fall between $1000 and $1200. It is interesting to note, however, that there is comparatively little change in the higher earnings groups. Somewhat in contrast to this the men tend to move up rather sharply in these groups. In this new classification practically one-fourth of all Hartford men are classified above $2000.

FAMILY INCOME

One of the subsidiary purposes of this study as originally planned was to make an analysis of family income, using the Company payroll data supplemented by information obtained in field interviews. It proved impossible, without unduly extending the time and expense of the field work, to get satisfactory statistical returns on this point. This would have involved obtaining payroll data from the employers of wage earners in the family other than those employed by the United States Rubber Company.

However, an attempt was made to obtain data on family income from the payroll records of the New Haven plant. Reference has been made to the great extent of family relationships existing among the workers there. On the basis of the personnel data available in Company records, forty-four families, represented by two or more wage earners in the New Haven plant, were selected for study. There were thirty-one men and sixty women included. Table 34 shows for each family the actual annual earnings for the individual workers as well as the total earnings for these members of the family.

This table shows the families arranged in ascending order of joint earnings. The first family consisting of a mother and her daughter received a total income from their rubber company jobs of $905.45. At the other extreme a sister and two brothers earned a family income of $4525.63. Likewise another group of three brothers earned $4249.11. The average joint earnings for this group of forty-four families amounted to $1937.61. This fairly well approximates the $2000 annual income which was at that time considered necessary for a decent standard of living. The average for the women was $749.10 and for the men $1300.28. The importance of additional wage earners in the family is strongly emphasized by these figures. The average joint earnings exceeded the average for the men alone by nearly 50 per cent.

A comparison of these figures with those given in Table 30 shows that the earnings of these workers were approximately on a level with the averages for the plant as a whole. It would seem, therefore, that the small sample above is not unrepresenta-

TABLE 34

Annual Incomes of Family Groups at New Haven Plant

Family No.	Relationship	Men	Women	Joint
Average		1300.28	749.10	1937.61
1	Mother, Daughter	......	117.11	
		......	788.34	905.45
2	Sisters	......	731.30	
		......	354.93	1086.23
3	Sisters	......	802.37	
		......	305.82	1108.19
4	Brother, Sister	227.44	887.83	1115.27
5	Sisters	......	549.49	
		......	732.30	1281.79
6	Sisters	......	471.65	
		......	875.37	1347.02
7	Husband, Wife	392.11	962.87	1354.98
8	Sisters	......	752.56	
		......	605.07	1357.63
9	Mother, Daughter	......	763.53	
		......	599.48	1363.01
10	Sisters	......	662.90	
		......	723.51	1386.41
11	Sisters	......	600.59	
		......	831.82	1432.41
12	Father, Daughter	1164.42	291.35	1455.77
13	Sisters	......	826.46	
		......	685.99	1512.45
14	Sisters	......	897.96	
		......	699.75	1597.71
15	Sisters	......	820.42	
		......	781.99	1602.41
16	Husband, Wife	1219.90	406.64	1626.54
17	Sisters	......	588.25	
		......	1070.30	1658.55
18	Sisters	......	832.55	
		......	832.19	1664.74
19	Sisters	......	736.69	
		......	932.30	1668.99
20	Husband, Wife	968.25	717.19	1685.44
21	Husband, Wife	1023.94	699.48	1723.42
22	Sisters	......	997.26	
		......	747.00	1744.26
23	Sisters	......	750.52	
		......	1003.52	1754.04
24	Sisters	......	923.62	
		......	848.15	1771.77
25	Mother, Daughter	......	1077.01	
		......	729.40	1806.41
26	Brother, Sister	1034.70	789.20	1823.90
27	Father, Daughter	1280.64	641.58	1922.22
28	Brother, Sister	1036.95	885.34	1922.29
29	Father, Daughter	1026.97	897.26	1924.23
30	Husband, Wife	1496.64	434.60	1931.24
31	Father, Daughter	1185.48	747.74	1933.22
32	Brother, Sister	848.56	1096.01	1944.57
33	Husband, Wife	1471.80	655.06	2126.86
34	Husband, Wife	1324.82	807.16	2131.98
35	Father, Daughters (Two)............	978.40	1039.89	
		......	290.14	2308.43
36	Husband, Wife	1433.97	884.72	2318.69
37	Husband, Daughter	1527.74	885.26	2413.00
38	Husband, Wife	1351.66	1071.24	2422.90
39	Husband, Wife	1712.74	879.18	2591.92
40	Father, Son	1737.50	......	
		925.93	......	2663.43
41	Brothers	1748.17	......	
		1515.39	......	3258.56
42	Father, Son	1960.29	......	
		1871.47	......	3831.76
43	Three Brothers	1800.86	......	
		871.70	......	
		1576.55	......	4249.11
44	Sister, Two Brothers...............	1943.01	......	
		1655.83	926.79	4525.63

tive. Since the families in the New Haven plant averaged 2.4 wage earners per family [1] it seems clear that, at the very minimum, family income would average more than 50 per cent in excess of the earnings of the individual male wage earners. Whatever may be the deficiencies in the above data (and they understate rather than overstate the case) it should be evident that cost of living comparisons for a family cannot be made on the basis of the earnings of individual wage earners. The only sound method would be to use the income supplied by all wage earners in the family. A great deal more information than is now available is needed on the subject of family income.

[1] See Table 19, p. 48.

APPENDIX B

SURVEY METHODS

Every effort was made to insure the highest possible degree of accuracy and reliability in the data collected in this study. At the very beginning of the survey the problem of the size of the staff arose. It was possible to have a larger staff covering the field work in a shorter time, or a smaller staff whose work would necesssarily have to be extended over a longer time. Conscious of the importance of the work in the field, we selected the latter alternative. The larger the number of interviewers, the more chance there would be for variation between them. With only three interviewers at work the problem of adjusting interpretations between them was a simple one. This method also gave opportunity for improvement and adaptation as the work proceeded. In other words, after a month's experience these three had the problem well in hand, while a dozen interviewers would by that time have completed the work. Hence the first step in obtaining a high quality of data was the restriction of the staff to a very small number of workers. The time element was not a factor of any consequence in the results.

The success or failure of a field study is to a very large extent determined by the staff of field workers. In this study too much credit can not be given to the three members of the staff who visited the families and collected the information. Doctor Vittorio Racca, formerly of the Universities of Rome and New York, had had research experience in Italy and the United States over a period of more than twenty-five years prior to his work on this study. He was able to reach Italian families who could not speak English. Mrs. Dorothy M. Tinklepaugh had a background of social work experience in California. Miss Harriet Adams, of New Haven, had for some years been engaged in work with young people, and was personally acquainted with many of the younger workers in the Candee plant. The conscientious and painstaking work of these staff members made

123

possible such results as were obtained in the field. They not
only gave freely of their time, working at nights and on holidays
and Sundays in order to reach the workers when they were
home, but they also took an active part in criticizing and devel-
oping the program.

Another problem was that involving the amount of information to be collected. In the beginning a more or less complete
summary of possible data was drawn up. Everything which
might have any relation to the subject was included. From that
point on a rigorous policy of exclusion and elimination was pur-
sued. Every item about which there was any question of un-
certainty was dropped or modified. What was left was then
cast into schedule form.

The drawing up of a schedule, however, did not complete the
process of revision. A preliminary schedule was drawn up and
actually used in the field for a week after which, in the light of
the field experience, certain further revisions were made and a
permanent schedule was determined upon. This was in New
Haven where the first survey was made. Subsequent experience
in New Haven made it apparent that certain questions were
not bringing in satisfactory answers. Therefore when the Candee
survey was completed and the Hartford work was ready, a new
draft was made, still further shortening the schedule and putting
it into more workable form for the interviewers. The two
schedules are shown on subsequent pages.

The third problem came to light in the tabulation of results.
Sometimes a question produced an answer without any kind of
difficulty but when the answers were tabulated they proved to be
of little significance. Thus Section II of the Candee schedule
was intended to develop some facts concerning methods used
by these families in looking for work. Answers were readily
obtained but the auditing of the schedules soon made it apparent that the data would be of little use for statistical purposes. The workers to a considerable extent had never heard of
employment offices and many of them did not read the papers;
they had only one standard method of looking for work. Under
the circumstances it was clear that pursuing the question further was simply wasting time and expense. Another illustration

INSTITUTE OF HUMAN RELATIONS, YALE UNIVERSITY   UNEMPLOYMENT SURVEY - HARTFORD RUBBER CO.

WORKER _____ REL. _____ AGE _____ NO. _____INVEST. _____

ADDRESS _____INTERVIEWED _____ DATE _____

1. EMPLOYMENT RECORD OF WORKER AND FAMILY (TO BE CARRIED AS FAR INTO THE PAST AS POSSIBLE)

| JOB (DESCRIBE) | FIRM (INDUSTRY) | HOW JOB OB'T'D | PERIOD | | | | PART TIME | REASON FOR LEAVING | EARNINGS | |
			AT WORK	FROM	TO	OUT OF WORK			FULL WK.	AV. WK.

AGE FIRST WENT TO WORK_____ HAS WORKER FOUND ANY JOB HE LIKES AS WELL AS HARTFORD RUBBER?_____

II. CHANGES IN LIVING CONDITIONS

1. PRESENT HOUSEHOLD — PARENTS, CHILDREN (AGES), OTHERS (ROOMERS) _____

CHANGES SINCE SEPTEMBER, 1929 _____

2. HOUSING:—TYPE _____ NO. ROOMS _____ HEAT _____ BATH _____MISC. _____ RATING _____

OWNED? _____ MORTGAGE _____ RENT PAID _____ RENT RECEIVED _____

3. SERIOUS ILLNESS OR ACCIDENT _____   4. INSURANCE:—IF NONE, WHY? _____

PERSON	DATES	DESCRIPTION	COST TO FAMILY	LOSS OF INCOME	PERSON	COMPANY	WEEKLY PREMIUM	POLICIES DROPPED

5. LOANS _____ 6. MISCELLANEOUS _____

| COMPANY | AMOUNT | REPAYMENTS | INT'ST RATE | PURPOSE | SALE OF PROPERTY | REPOS-SESSION | INCOME | | | |
							RELATIVE	PENSION	CHARITY	OTHER

III. TERMINATION WAGE OR PENSION (IF ANY):—AMOUNT _____

PROPORTION SPENT _____ HOW — RUNNING EXPENSES, BACK DEBTS, INSTALLMENTS _____

ANY SAVED OR INVESTED? _____ HOW?_____

HOW MUCH STILL READILY AVAILABLE TO FAMILY? _____

SCHEDULE USED IN HARTFORD

occurs in insurance. The families did not know what kind of a policy they had or what its face value was. They did know whether they paid by the week, by the month, or by some longer period, and they also knew what the premiums were. From these premium payments it was possible to estimate the face value of the policies with greater accuracy than the families could report on them. There were a number of other instances

INSTITUTE OF HUMAN RELATIONS   Survey of Workers laid off by
Yale University   L. Candee Company Shutdown

Worker.. Investigator.............................. Dates......................

Address .... Person interviewed...

I. *Employment Record of Worker and Family* (to be carried as far back as possible)

Person	Job (describe)	Industry	Firm	PERIOD			Per Am't
				time	to	from	

I. (con.) Age first went to work............................ Why (if under 16)................................

WEEKLY HOURS		HOW OBTAINED JOB		Reason for Leaving	EARNINGS			
Reg.	Usual	Method	Cost		Hour	Full Week	Av. Week	Total

Has worker found any job he likes as well as Candee?...
SCHEDULE USED IN NEW HAVEN

II. *Methods of Finding Work* (whole family)

    1. Employment offices—(a) private, (b) public, (c) organization; 2. Newspaper ads.—(a) help wanted, (b) situation wanted; 3. Application at plant; 4. Fellow workers; 5. Other methods.

Person	Period	Methods	Reasons for Not Getting Jobs	REASONS FOR NOT USING				
				Private Empl. Off.	Public Empl. Off.	Organ. Empl. Off.	Help Wanted	Sit'n Wanted

III. *Changes in Living Conditions*

    1. Present household—parents, children (ages), other (roomers).................

....

    Changes since March, 1929...

    (dates if possible)...

    2. Housing: Type and size...

    Owned?.....................Mortgage interest...................Rent paid.................

    Rent rec'd...........................Moved since March, 1929?.........................

    Dates.................. Reasons...

    3. Serious illness or accident.

Person	DATES		Description	Cost to Family	Loss of Income
	From	To			

    4. Insurance. If none in family, why not?...

Person	Kind of Policy	Company	Date	Face Value	Premium Paid	Policies Dropped Since March, 1929
Total						

    5. Financial

    Any loans recently?...................Company.............................Amount...................

    Interest...............................Amount outstanding...

    General ....

    Sale of property—land, house, car...................Instalment foreclosure.......................

    Income—relatives..................... pensions.................charity...................other...............

....

IV. *Termination wage or pension,* (if any)   Amount...

    Spent...................... How—running exp., back debts, instalments.........................

    Invested............................ How...

    How much still readily available...

SCHEDULE USED IN NEW HAVEN
(Page 2)

of items for which the reports either were colorless or valueless so that no attempt was made to tabulate them.

A final problem was that of the accuracy and reliability of the data reported by the family to the interviewer. It was not practicable to check up through outside sources on many of the statements and therefore some method had to be devised for testing each schedule. The simplest test is that of internal consistency, therefore each schedule as it came in was carefully audited to make sure that all the facts hung together. Another method which naturally suggested itself was that of using the information already available to us in the reports of the United States Rubber Company. All significant data about the worker and the family were listed in advance of the interview and the field worker familiarized himself with these facts before making the visit. Then the schedule was drawn up in such a way that the worker was required to state in his own language the facts about his United States Rubber Company job. Thus on Page 1 of the schedule the worker gave his employment record as far back as he could remember; in that process he naturally included his Candee or Hartford rubber works job. The worker's own report was then compared, item by item, with the Company's records.[1] By means of these comparisons we were able to determine the reliability, not only of the schedule as a whole, but of certain types of answers.

---

[1] Factory records, although they are the basic source of data for this type of statistical study, frequently present serious difficulties. In this case a great deal of the information was as of the date of hiring or of last re-hiring; thus any facts which might vary with time, such as the number and kinds of dependents, citizenship, etc., were subject to the danger of being out of date. Again, the management's appraisal of the worker, embodied in such records as previous employer, length of service, absenteeism, etc., was often incomplete to an uncertain and indefinite extent. Or, to consider still another aspect, management rules and definitions with reference to length of service, skill rating, etc., sometimes proved too rigid and formal for research purposes and had to be modified in order to obtain a better expression of the workers' point of view. Thus, length of service might be defined as (1) the entire period elapsed since the worker first joined the company, regardless of intermediate absences, (2) the total actual *working* time put in by the worker since he was first hired, or (3) the official company record of working time, counting only the period since the last break in service; the latter often falls far short of expressing the full period worked by the employee. Finally, of course, on some types of company ratings the standards were greatly relaxed at the time of closing, chiefly in those respects which might influence the worker's chances of getting a job. The foremen's grading on quantity, quality, attitude and attendance proved so high as to be unreliable.

As a result of these tests we have come to the following conclusions. A vast majority of the workers answer as accurately
as they are able to do so. Only a very small fraction of the
schedules gave evidence of attempts to mislead the interviewers.
Rarely a whole schedule will be so incorrect as to necessitate
rejection. In other cases the inaccuracy was confined to certain
questions, although the attempt to mislead and the bias back
of it was apparent. In the whole number involved the proportion of schedules of this type was negligible.

On the other hand there is no doubt that on certain points
the worker can give better answers than on others. The replies
with respect to wage rates were on the whole excellent. In many
cases, even after a year had elapsed, the worker's estimate of his
average full time earnings with the rubber company came within
a fraction of a dollar of those computed by us from his payroll
record. On time intervals, however, he is much less sure of
himself. In reporting on the length of time worked he tends to
answer in round numbers, and also to ignore minor interruptions.
Some workers gave ten years as their length of service with the
rubber company when, as a matter of fact, they had been there
only about nine years, and during this time they had been away
for several months on one or two occasions. There is no doubt
that the workers' estimates on their time out of work are subject to a certain amount of correction for inaccuracy. In every
possible way the interviewers endeavored to help the worker in
his time estimates. They used such devices as connecting the
job or the unemployment with certain specific dates, such as
Christmas, Thanksgiving, etc. On the whole the data as presented in this study are accurate, and if the necessary corrections
could be made the results would not be materially changed.
Nevertheless it is our duty to report that the tables as shown
may contain certain minor errors.

APPENDIX C

COMMUNITY ACTION IN HARTFORD

Although the Hartford shutdown occurred at a time when economic conditions were rapidly becoming unfavorable, the displaced workers had the benefit of a well-planned and most effective drive for jobs. So complete was the coöperation achieved that the entire community began functioning almost as a unit in the interests of the unemployed ex-rubber workers. The Common Council of Hartford, at its first meeting following announcement of the shutdown, passed a resolution requesting Mayor Batterson to "advise the City Unemployment Committee to coöperate with the officials of the Hartford Rubber Works Company in an effort to secure employment for those who find themselves unemployed due to the closing."[1] The Mayor had already appointed a special committee to consider the unemployment situation in Hartford. At the next meeting of this committee the ground work was laid for a campaign to provide employment for the entire working force laid off (about 1400 men). The committee adopted the recommendation of Mr. T. J. Kelley, then secretary of the Hartford County Manufacturers Association, that the employment office of the Hartford Rubber Works be continued indefinitely as a clearing house for jobs. The committee further made plans to protect such of the workers as might be harassed by credit establishments for loans contracted without the knowledge that they would be laid off. They planned to take up with the banks, credit associations and loan organizations the matter of extending credit to rubber workers with good records; this same policy was to be followed for automobile concerns, house furnishings stores and merchants generally.

These moves were followed by a policy of wide-spread publicity. The employment department of the rubber works prepared a list of the employes classified by skill and by nationality,

[1] Hartfort Courant, August 20, 1929.

showing name, age, citizenship, marital status, dependents, service, weekly rate of pay, type of job, place of residence, and ability to read and write English. This list showed two employes classified as skilled in metal work, 17 semi-skilled in metal, 856 especially skilled in rubber work but readily adaptable to other jobs with some training, and finally, 138 workers classified as unskilled labor. This list was sent to all leading employers in the city. Then the Mayor's Unemployment Committee published advertisements in the newspapers. The following is a sample:

EMPLOYMENT WANTED

Business concerns, factories and citizens are urged to telephone their labor requirements to the labor department of the Hartford Rubber Works, and we urge them to give preference in employment, during the existing crisis, insofar as it is technically possible to employes of this company and particularly to residents of Hartford who are responsible for the support of dependents. To insure proper identification, introduction cards will be issued to the men sent on jobs.

MAYOR'S UNEMPLOYMENT COMMITTEE[1]

The wording of these advertisements was changed from time to time, the last one issued toward the end of September being entitled,

A FINAL APPEAL

Approximately 600 of the former Rubber Works' employees have been placed as a result of the splendid coöperation of our employers with Mayor Batterson's Unemployment Committee. There is still a relatively small number to be placed and in their interests we make a final and earnest appeal. Let's make a 100 per cent rating in this situation and by so doing record an outstanding example of civic coöperation in the solution of what appeared to be a serious community unemployment problem.[2]

Finally the newspapers themselves gave assistance to the workers in their hunt for jobs. The following announcement was published in the *Hartford Times:*

HARTFORD RUBBER WORKS EMPLOYEES

The Hartford Times is anxious to lend its facilities to aid in placing you in other positions in and around Hartford. It has offered the use of its advertising and news columns without any charge to the Mayor's Unemployment Committee. This offer has been thankfully acknowledged by the Committee which is acting in your interests. The Times sincerely hopes that you will be able to find employment in other industries or business houses of this splendid city of ours, and that you will not be forced to seek employment in other fields.[3]

[1] Hartford Times, September 9th, 1929.
[2] Hartford Times, September 24th, 1929.
[3] September 5, 1929.

Other steps taken in the city were summarized in a report by Mr. Kelley, the Secretary of the Manufacturers Association:

"The contractors of the city of Hartford have offered, voluntarily, to restrict their recruiting of rough labor to former unskilled employees of the Hartford Rubber Works until such employees have been absorbed.

"The park, street and aviation commissioners of the city, at the request of the Mayor, are now investigating to see what work can be undertaken with a view to relieving the immediate situation.

"The electric light company has given instructions that for the present, so far as is technically possible, employment of new help be restricted to former employees of the Hartford Rubber Works. The Board of Directors of this company has also called a special meeting to consider the question of undertaking work that otherwise would not be commenced until next spring, with a view to relieving the immediate unemployment tension."

Undoubtedly this drive for jobs, and the excellent publicity which accompanied it, accomplished a great deal. Many men were successfully placed very soon after the lay-off. It gave to the others who were still seeking work, the assurance that the community as a whole was back of them and was working for them. This assurance of support was unquestionably a source of confidence to many workers.

The dismissal wage payments, made to 126 workers and amounting to over $100,000 in the total, had the same effect upon the attitude of the employes toward the company as had existed in New Haven. There is evidence, however, of some dissatisfaction among the men. At the time of the closing a Rubber Workers Relief Committee was formed at a meeting of approximately 100 of the Company employes.[1] The Committee planned to petition the Company for three months' pay for every employe in the shop plus pensions for all employes over 40. The city and state governments were to be requested to aid in finding positions. The newspaper report suggests that this committee had been organized by the Communists, but this is not certain. At any rate apparently nothing came of it.

Despite all these vigorous efforts of the community in coöperation with the company, the final results, so far as the workers themselves were concerned, were not especially different from those in New Haven, as will be seen from the analysis of the figures. The reason was simple. In New Haven business conditions remained moderately good throughout the summer and

[1] Hartford Times, August 26, 1929.

therefore the workers, even without much outside help, were able to find jobs. In Hartford scarcely a month had passed after the shutdown when a terrific set-back occurred in general business. Plants began laying off instead of hiring, and placement of the rubber workers came almost to a standstill by the end of September. Furthermore, some of the workers placed had scarcely begun work when they were laid off by the new employer. Being the last hired they were the first to go in the reduction of working force. The Hartford community had done everything that seemed possible under the circumstances and they are to be heartily commended for their vigorous coöperative action; it was not the fault of the community that the effort to place all workers in new permanent jobs was not wholly successful.

APPENDIX D
SUPPLEMENTARY TABLES
PART I

TABLE 35—H.

Length of Time Necessary to Find Work

Showing number of months to first permanent job, by age groups

HARTFORD

Age Groups	Total	Number of Months												Did Not Find	Did Not Look
		0	1	2	3	4	5	6	7	8	9	10	Un-known		
Total	*534*	*154*	*95*	*56*	*33*	*29*	*13*	*18*	*14*	*12*	*11*	*5*	*2*	*83*	*9*
15–19	11	3	2	..	..	1	..	1	..	..	..	..	..	2	2
20–24	46	15	7	3	3	3	1	2	2	..	2	1	..	6	1
25–29	80	28	15	10	4	3	2	4	1	2	1	..	..	10	..
30–34	91	26	19	11	11	4	2	1	1	2	4	..	1	9	..
35–39	109	28	20	14	5	9	1	6	2	2	3	2	1	16	..
40–44	88	30	14	6	4	6	4	1	3	1	..	2	..	17	..
45–49	50	15	8	5	5	1	1	2	3	2	..	..	..	8	..
50–54	26	4	7	3	..	2	1	1	2	2	..	..	..	4	..
55–59	14	3	3	3	..	..	..	..	..	..	1	..	..	3	1
60–64	9	2	..	1	..	..	..	..	..	..	..	..	..	5	1
65–69	3	..	..	..	1	..	1	..	..	1	..	..	..	1	..
Pensions	7	..	..	..	..	..	1	..	..	..	..	..	..	2	4

TABLE 35—N.

Length of Time Necessary to Find Work

Showing number of months to first permanent job, by age groups

NEW HAVEN

Age Groups	Total	Number of Months													Did Not Find	Did Not Look
		0	1	2	3	4	5	6	7	8	9	10	11	Un-known		
a. Men																
Total	*244*	*70*	*44*	*26*	*18*	*9*	*6*	*11*	*5*	*4*	*5*	*2*	*..*	*1*	*28*	*15*
15–19	24	8	6	3	1	1	..	0	1	1	0	1	..	..	1	1
20–24	18	4	4	2	3	..	1	3	..	..	1	..	..	..	..	..
25–29	26	9	3	5	..	2	1	1	..	1	1	..	..	..	3	..
30–34	28	12	5	2	3	2	..	3	..	..	1	..	..	..	..	..
35–39	23	9	5	1	4	1	..	1	..	..	..	..	..	..	2	..
40–44	32	12	9	8	1	1	..	..	1	..	..	..	..	..	..	..
45–49	32	8	5	2	4	..	1	..	1	2	1	1	..	1	5	1
50–54	19	4	5	2	1	..	..	1	..	..	..	..	..	..	6	..
55–59	16	3	..	1	..	2	2	..	..	..	1	..	..	..	6	1
60–64	9	1	1	..	..	..	..	1	1	..	..	..	..	..	2	3
65–69	1	..	1	..	..	..	..	..	..	..	..	..	..	..	..	..
Pensions	16	..	..	..	1	..	..	1	2	..	..	..	..	..	3	9
b. Women																
Total	*428*	*147*	*61*	*23*	*25*	*13*	*11*	*10*	*4*	*12*	*5*	*6*	*1*	*1*	*40*	*69*
15–19	79	31	19	8	5	1	3	1	..	1	2	..	1	..	5	2
20–24	81	43	8	3	8	4	2	1	..	1	1	1	..	..	3	6
25–29	79	32	11	4	2	4	1	..	1	5	1	2	..	..	9	7
30–34	43	15	6	3	1	1	..	..	1	1	..	1	..	1	4	9
35–39	43	9	4	1	2	1	3	3	1	1	..	1	..	..	9	8
40–44	38	12	6	..	2	1	..	2	..	1	..	1	..	..	5	8
45–49	20	3	4	1	3	..	1	2	..	1	1	..	..	..	1	3
50–54	14	..	3	2	2	..	1	..	1	..	..	..	..	..	1	4
55–59	5	..	..	1	..	..	..	..	..	..	..	..	..	..	..	4
60–64	1	..	..	..	..	..	..	..	1	..	..	..	..	..	..	..
65–69	..	..	..	..	..	..	..	..	..	..	..	..	..	..	..	..
Pensions	25	2	..	..	..	1	..	1	..	..	..	..	..	..	3	18

TABLE 36—H.

Length of Time on First Permanent Job

Showing number of months such jobs were held, by age groups

HARTFORD

Age Groups	Total Number Finding Permanent Jobs	Number of months on Job											Survey Date	Un-known
		0	1	2	3	4	5	6	7	8	9	10		
Total	*442*	*21*	*48*	*36*	*30*	*15*	*15*	*6*	*8*	*4*	*4*	*1*	*253*	*1*
15–19	7	1	1	1	..	..	..	1	..	1	..	..	2	..
20–24	39	2	5	2	2	1	1	..	3	1	1	1	20	..
25–29	70	1	10	2	4	2	3	..	1	1	..	..	46	..
30–34	82	4	11	5	8	3	4	3	1	1	..	..	41	1
35–39	93	3	8	13	7	3	3	1	1	..	..	..	54	..
40–44	71	4	9	5	5	..	1	..	..	..	1	..	46	..
45–49	42	4	2	4	2	5	3	1	..	..	1	..	20	..
50–54	22	1	2	3	2	..	..	..	1	..	..	..	13	..
55–59	10	1	..	1	..	1	..	..	..	..	1	..	6	..
60–64	3	..	..	..	..	..	..	1	..	..	..	..	2	..
65–69	2	..	..	..	..	..	..	..	..	..	..	..	2	..
Pensions	1	..	..	..	..	..	..	..	..	..	..	..	1	..

TABLE 36—N.

Length of Time on First Permanent Job

Showing number of months such jobs were held, by age groups

NEW HAVEN

Age Groups	Total Number Finding Permanent Jobs	Number of Months on Job												Survey Date	Un-known
		0	1	2	3	4	5	6	7	8	9	10	11		
a. Men															
Total	*210*	*17*	*15*	*24*	*15*	*5*	*9*	*8*	*1*	*4*	*2*	..	..	*100*	*1*
15–19	22	2	2	5	2	..	1	2	1	..	..	..	..	7	..
20–24	18	5	2	1	3	..	1	1	..	..	..	..	..	5	..
25–29	23	2	2	2	1	..	3	..	..	..	..	..	..	13	..
30–34	28	1	4	7	1	1	..	1	..	1	..	..	..	13	1
35–39	21	2	..	5	..	..	..	1	..	1	..	..	..	11	..
40–44	32	3	1	3	2	1	..	1	..	3	1	..	..	17	..
45–49	26	1	3	..	2	2	1	1	..	..	1	..	..	15	..
50–54	13	1	..	1	2	..	2	1	..	..	..	..	..	6	..
55–59	9	..	1	..	1	1	..	..	..	..	..	..	..	6	..
60–64	4	..	..	..	..	..	1	..	..	..	..	..	..	3	..
65–69	1	..	..	..	1	..	..	..	..	..	..	..	..	..	..
Pensions	4	..	..	..	..	..	..	..	..	..	..	..	..	4	..
b. Women															
Total	*319*	*42*	*41*	*23*	*19*	*12*	*11*	*15*	*4*	*5*	*4*	*2*	..	*140*	*1*
15–19	72	4	10	3	3	4	6	8	2	1	2	..	..	29	..
20–24	72	18	8	8	5	2	..	2	1	2	1	2	..	23	..
25–29	63	7	8	..	5	4	1	..	1	1	1	..	..	35	..
30–34	30	2	5	5	1	..	1	2	..	..	..	..	..	13	1
35–39	26	4	5	3	1	..	..	1	..	..	..	..	..	12	..
40–44	25	4	3	3	2	1	..	2	..	..	..	..	..	10	..
45–49	16	2	1	..	..	1	3	..	..	..	..	..	..	9	..
50–54	9	..	..	1	2	..	..	..	..	1	..	..	..	5	..
55–59	1	..	1	..	..	..	..	..	..	..	..	..	..	..	..
60–64	1	..	..	..	..	..	..	..	..	..	..	..	..	1	..
65–69	..	..	..	..	..	..	..	..	..	..	..	..	..	..	..
Pensions	4	1	..	..	..	..	..	..	..	..	..	..	..	3	..

TABLE 37—H.

Total Amount of Working Time Lost by Those Seeking Work, by Age Groups

HARTFORD

Age Groups	Total Number Seeking Work	Number of Months Lost												Entire Period Lost—Did Not Find Work
		0	1	2	3	4	5	6	7	8	9	10	Unknown	
Total	*534*	*108*	*64*	*53*	*35*	*20*	*38*	*30*	*31*	*41*	*50*	*7*	*7*	*50*
15–19	11	1	1	1	..	1	..	..	..	3	..	..	..	4
20–24	46	10	6	2	2	2	4	3	1	2	5	3	3	3
25–29	80	19	12	12	4	3	5	4	5	7	7	..	..	2
30–34	91	20	12	9	8	3	5	5	7	9	8	..	1	4
35–39	109	20	14	16	3	6	6	7	7	10	13	2	1	4
40–44	88	26	6	5	4	4	10	3	3	3	7	1	1	15
45–49	50	9	6	4	8	..	4	4	4	3	4	..	1	3
50–54	26	1	4	1	3	1	3	2	4	2	4	..	1	1
55–59	14	1	3	3	..	..	..	2	..	..	..	1	..	4
60–64	9	1	..	..	2	..	..	..	..	..	..	..	..	6
65–69	3	..	..	..	1	..	..	..	..	1	1	..	..	..
Pensions	7	..	..	..	..	..	..	1	..	..	1	1	..	4

TABLE 37—N.

Total Amount of Working Time Lost by Those Seeking Work, by Age Groups

NEW HAVEN

Age Groups	Total Number Seeking Work	Number of Months Lost													Entire Period Lost—Did Not Find Work
		0	1	2	3	4	5	6	7	8	9	10	11	Unknown	
a. Men															
Total	*244*	*51*	*29*	*25*	*23*	*11*	*7*	*19*	*8*	*17*	*9*	*8*	*4*	*2*	*31*
15–19	24	3	2	3	1	3	1	3	..	5	1	1	1	..	..
20–24	18	2	4	1	..	1	1	3	..	4	..	1	1	..	..
25–29	26	7	1	7	3	1	..	1	..	1	2	1	..	..	2
30–34	28	8	6	1	3	1	..	4	..	2	3	..	..	..	..
35–39	23	8	3	2	5	1	..	..	2	..	1	..	..	1	..
40–44	32	12	4	8	3	2	1	1	1	..	..	..	..	..	..
45–49	32	7	5	1	3	..	2	2	1	1	2	2	2	1	3
50–54	19	2	3	1	3	..	1	2	..	1	..	1	..	..	5
55–59	16	1	..	1	1	2	1	..	1	3	..	2	..	..	4
60–64	9	1	1	..	..	..	..	2	..	..	..	..	..	..	5
65–69	1	..	..	..	..	..	..	..	1	..	..	..	..	..	..
Pensions	16	..	..	..	1	..	..	1	2	..	..	..	..	..	12
b. Women															
Total	*428*	*80*	*42*	*31*	*20*	*24*	*13*	*24*	*15*	*26*	*14*	*24*	*12*	*2*	*101*
15–19	79	20	10	13	4	7	4	3	1	6	3	1	3	..	4
20–24	81	22	7	7	5	8	1	4	6	2	3	3	3	1	9
25–29	79	19	10	3	6	4	..	2	2	7	2	8	1	..	15
30–34	43	7	2	1	..	1	3	2	3	5	1	3	1	1	13
35–39	43	4	4	2	..	1	3	4	1	2	4	2	1	..	15
40–44	38	5	3	2	3	2	1	3	..	2	..	2	2	..	13
45–49	20	1	4	3	..	..	..	3	1	1	1	3	..	..	3
50–54	14	..	2	..	2	1	1	1	1	1	..	1	..	..	4
55–59	5	..	..	..	..	..	..	1	..	..	..	1	..	..	4
60–64	1	..	..	..	..	..	..	1	..	..	..	..	..	..	..
65–69	..	..	..	..	..	..	..	..	..	..	..	..	..	..	..
Pensions	25	2	..	..	..	..	..	1	..	..	..	..	..	1	21

TABLE 38—II.

Employment on Closing Date of Survey

Showing number of workers holding permanent jobs on July 1, 1930, by age groups

HARTFORD

Age Groups	Total Number of Workers	Status on July 1, 1930		Not Looking for Work	Unknown
		Holding Permanent Job	Unemployed		
Total	*534*	*364*	*159*	*11*	..
15–19	11	3	6	2	..
20–24	46	30	15	1	..
25–29	80	64	15	1	..
30–34	91	64	27	..	..
35–39	109	81	28	..	..
40–44	88	57	31	..	..
45–49	50	35	15	..	..
50–54	26	18	8	..	..
55–59	14	7	5	2	..
60–64	9	2	6	1	..
65–69	3	2	1	..	..
Pensions	7	1	2	4	..

TABLE 38—N.

Employment on Closing Date of Survey

Showing number of workers holding permanent jobs on March 1, 1930, by age groups

NEW HAVEN

Age Groups	Total Number of Workers	Status on March 1, 1930		Not Looking for Work	Unknown
		Holding Permanent Job	Unemployed		
a. *Men*					
Total	*244*	*158*	*69*	*17*	..
15–19	24	13	10	1	..
20–24	18	10	8	..	..
25–29	26	21	5	..	..
30–34	28	23	4	1	..
35–39	23	19	4	..	..
40–44	32	29	3	..	..
45–49	32	21	10	1	..
50–54	19	9	10	..	..
55–59	16	6	8	2	..
60–64	9	3	3	3	..
65–69	1	..	1	..	..
Pensions	16	4	3	9	..
b. *Women*					
Total	*428*	*247*	*76*	*104*	*1*
15–19	79	58	13	8	..
20–24	81	56	11	13	1
25–29	79	51	12	16	..
30–34	43	19	8	16	..
35–39	43	22	11	10	..
40–44	38	19	8	11	..
45–49	20	12	5	3	..
50–54	14	6	4	4	..
55–59	5	..	..	5	..
60–64	1	1	..	..	..
65–69	..	..	..	..	..
Pensions	25	3	4	18	..

After the Shutdown

TABLE 39—H.

Percentage Changes in Wage Rates

Best-paid job found as compared with Hartford Rubber job, by age groups

Age Groups	Total Number Reporting Comparable Data	INCREASE				No Change	Change Unknown*	DECREASE							
		30–39%	20–29%	10–19%	0–9%			0–9%	10–19%	20–29%	30–39%	40–49%	50–59%	60–69%	70–79%
Total	420	1	1	7	8	19	15	36	48	68	113	72	23	8	1
15–19	7	..	..	1	1	..	..	1	1	1	2	..	..	..	..
20–24	35	..	1	..	1	..	2	6	3	8	7	5	2	..	..
25–29	68	..	..	1	2	2	..	7	11	10	22	8	4	1	..
30–34	81	..	..	4	1	7	1	7	10	9	23	9	7	2	1
35–39	88	1	..	1	1	6	7	1	3	20	28	16	3	1	..
40–44	64	..	..	..	1	2	2	6	7	9	19	14	3	1	..
45–49	41	..	..	..	1	2	..	7	6	6	7	8	3	1	..
50–54	20	..	..	..	..	..	1	2	2	3	2	8	1	1	..
55–59	10	..	..	..	..	..	1	..	4	..	4	1	..	..	..
60–64	3	..	..	..	..	..	..	..	1	1	..	..	..	1	..
65–69	2	..	..	..	..	..	1	..	..	1	..	..	..	..	..
Pensions	1	..	..	..	..	..	..	..	..	..	..	1	..	..	..

* Includes increases unknown, decreases unknown, and change unknown.

TABLE 39—N.

Percentage Changes in Wage Rates

Best-paid job found as compared with Candee Rubber job, by age groups

Age Groups	Total Number Reporting Comparable Data	Over 100%	INCREASE								No Change	Change Unknown*	DECREASE							
			80–89%	60–69%	50–59%	40–49%	30–39%	20–29%	10–19%	0–9%			0–9%	10–19%	20–29%	30–39%	40–49%	50–59%	60–69%	70–79%
a. Men																				
Total	191	3	1	4	3	3	5	4	4	12	21	5	11	24	24	31	21	9	3	2
15–19	22	3	..	2	3	1	..	..	..	2	1	..	2	2	2	1	1	1	..	..
20–24	18	..	1	..	..	..	2	1	..	2	3	..	1	3	2	1	..	2	..	..
25–29	23	..	..	2	..	..	1	1	..	2	..	2	3	4	1	3	4	..	..	..
30–34	27	..	..	..	..	..	2	1	1	4	..	1	4	2	8	3	1	..	..	..
35–39	18	..	..	..	..	..	..	..	..	3	1	2	2	4	3	2	..	1	..	..
40–44	29	..	..	..	..	..	1	..	2	3	..	2	3	5	6	4	1	..	..	..
45–49	24	..	..	..	..	1	..	1	1	4	1	..	5	1	5	2	3	..	..	..
50–54	13	..	..	..	..	1	..	..	..	1	1	..	..	3	3	3	..	1	..	..
55–59	9	..	..	..	..	..	..	..	..	1	..	..	1	3	1	1	1	1	..	..
60–64	3	..	..	..	..	1	..	..	..	..	..	..	..	1	..	1	..	..	..	..
65–69	1	..	..	..	..	..	..	..	..	..	..	1	..	..	..	..	..	..	..	..
Pensions	4	..	..	..	..	..	..	..	..	1	1	..	..	..	..	..	..	..	..	2
b. Women		(80–89)%	(70–79)%																	
Total	311	2	2	4	2	5	13	4	12	7	24	6	21	44	37	42	39	24	16	7
15–19	72	2	..	2	1	2	4	2	6	2	11	..	6	9	10	8	6	1	..	..
20–24	69	..	..	1	..	1	..	1	1	..	8	1	7	16	8	4	13	3	2	3
25–29	59	..	2	..	..	2	1	2	2	..	..	..	..	10	9	14	6	9	2	..
30–34	30	..	..	1	..	2	1	..	2	2	2	1	2	3	1	4	3	3	3	..
35–39	26	..	..	..	..	1	1	1	..	1	2	1	3	3	4	3	6	1	..	..
40–44	25	..	..	..	1	1	1	..	2	..	..	..	3	3	2	5	3	1	2	1
45–49	16	..	..	1	1	1	1	..	..	..	..	..	..	4	3	1	1	1	2	..
50–54	8	..	..	1	..	1	..	1	1	..	2	..	..	1	1	..	..	..	..	..
55–59	1	..	..	..	1	..	..	..	..	..	..	..	..	..	..	..	..	..	..	..
60–64	1	..	..	..	..	..	..	..	..	..	..	1	..	..	..	..	..	..	..	..
Pensions	4	..	..	..	..	..	..	..	..	..	..	..	..	1	1	..	..	2	..	..

* Includes increase unknown, decrease unknown, and change unknown.

TABLE 40—N.

Working Time Lost by New Haven Workers During Eleven Months' Period Following Shutdown

(Expressed in percentages of total time)

AGE GROUPS	MEN			WOMEN		
	Total Number Looking for Work	Average Number of Months Lost	Ratio: Months Lost to Total Months (11 Per Cent)	Total Number Looking for Work	Average Number of Months Lost	Ratio: Months Lost to Total Months (11 Per Cent)
Total	*228*	*4.1*	*36.9*	*358*	*4.6*	*41.7*
15–19	24	4.8	43.9	77	3.4	30.8
20–24	18	4.8	43.5	74	3.7	33.3
25–29	26	3.5	32.2	72	4.6	41.5
30–34	28	3.1	28.5	33	5.8	52.4
35–39	22	2.2	20.3	36	6.4	57.8
40–44	32	1.7	15.6	30	5.3	48.5
45–49	30	4.5	40.9	17	4.8	43.8
50–54	19	5.5	49.7	10	4.8	43.6
55–59	15	6.8	61.8	1	10.0	90.9
60–64	6	5.8	53.0	1	6.0	54.5
65–69	1	7.0	63.6	..	..	...
Pensioners	7	8.0	72.7	7	7.1	64.9

TABLE 41—N.

Annual Earnings of New Haven Workers, 1929–1930

(Expressed in percentage of 1928 annual earnings)

AGE GROUPS	MEN		WOMEN	
	Number of* Workers Reporting Comparable Earnings	1929–30 Earnings in Percentages (1928=100)	Number of* Workers Reporting Comparable Earnings	1929–30 Earnings in Percentages (1928=100)
Total	*188*	*53.6*	*316*	*51.8*
15–19	15	54.0	60	73.1
20–24	16	57.1	69	56.3
25–29	21	59.8	65	49.2
30–34	25	57.7	32	54.3
35–39	17	60.6	33	27.2
40–44	27	65.4	30	43.7
45–49	28	52.5	17	46.5
50–54	19	40.8	9	48.6
55–59	15	29.4	1	9.5
60–64	5	29.2	..	...

* Excluding those whose complete 1928 earnings could not be obtained; also those later engaged in business for themselves, those not looking for work, etc., etc.

APPENDIX E
TABLES
PART II

TABLE 42

Summary of Cases

	MEN					WOMEN				
AGE GROUPS*	Total Schedules	Working or Seeking Work	Pensioned	Not Seeking Work	Own Business	Total Schedules	Working or Seeking Work	Pensioned	Not Seeking Work	Own Business
15–19	18	17	0	1	0	58	50	0	8	0
20–24	14	14	0	0	0	57	36	0	20	1
25–29	19	18	0	0	1	60	43	0	16	1
30–34	24	23	0	0	1	33	15	0	18	0
35–39	18	15	0	1	2	34	23	0	11	0
40–44	29	27	0	0	2	30	18	0	12	0
45–49	21	15	0	2	4	18	12	0	5	1
50–54	12	11	0	0	1	14	5	2	6	1
55–59	14	12	1	0	1	15	2	10	3	0
60–64	15	5	6	3	1	8	0	6	2	0
65–69	8	1	6	1	0	3	0	3	0	0
70–74	1	0	1	0	0	0	0	0	0	0
Total	193**	158	14	8	13	330**	204	21	101	4

* The ages used for the former survey by Messrs. Clague and Couper are retained for classifying the workers in this survey, so that the age groups contain identical individuals so far as we were able to locate them.

** Of the 672 workers for whom schedules were obtained in the first survey, 523 gave satisfactory information in 1932. The other cases are accounted for as follows: died, 10; could not be located, 27; definite information indicating removal to another city, 41; refused information, 24; in jail, 2; total 149.

TABLE 43

Extent of Unemployment

(Expressed as average months and per cent of total time unemployed for those seeking work in each year, and annual average for the three-year period 4-'29 to 4-'32)

	EXTENT OF UNEMPLOYMENT			
	158 MEN		204 WOMEN	
YEAR	Average Months Unemployed	Per Cent of Time Unemployed	Average Months Unemployed	Per Cent of Time Unemployed
4-'29 to 4-'30	4.3	35.5	4.7	39.2
4-'30 to 4-'31	3.9	33.2	3.5	29.3
4-'31 to 4-'32	4.8	40.2	3.8	31.3
Annual Average, *4-'29 to 4-'32*	*4.4*	*36.3*	*4.0*	*33.2*

TABLE 44

Extent of Unemployment

(Expressed as average months per annum and per cent of time unemployed for those seeking work for the three-year period 4-'29 to 4-'32, classified according to age groups)

AGE GROUPS	MEN			WOMEN		
		EXTENT OF UNEMPLOYMENT			EXTENT OF UNEMPLOYMENT	
	Number Seeking Work	Average Months Unemployed Per Annum 4-'29 to 4-'32	Per Cent of Time Unemployed 4-'29 to 4-'32	Number Seeking Work	Average Months Unemployed Per Annum 4-'29 to 4-'32	Per Cent of Time Unemployed 4-'29 to 4-'32
15–19	17	4.1	34.2	50	3.1	25.5
20–24	14	5.3	44.3	36	3.4	28.1
25–29	18	5.2	43.7	43	3.7	31.2
30–34	23	2.6	21.3	15	4.9	41.2
35–39	15	2.7	22.7	23	6.1	50.8
40–44	27	2.6	21.9	18	4.7	39.1
45–49	15	4.6	38.5	12	2.2	18.5
50–54	11	7.2	59.9	5	5.9	49.2
55–59	12	7.2	60.4	2	11.9	98.9
60–64	5	8.4	70.3	0	...	...
65–69	1	1.7	13.9	0	...	...
70–74	0	..	...	0	...	...
Average	158	4.4	36.3	204	4.0	33.2

TABLE 45

Average Annual Earnings of Those Working and Seeking Work, for 1928, for Each Year, and for Three-Year Period 4-'29 to 4-'32

(Expressed as amounts and percentages of 1928 earnings)

YEAR	AVERAGE ANNUAL EARNINGS			
	158 MEN		204 WOMEN	
	Amount	Per Cent of 1928 Earnings	Amount	Per Cent of 1928 Earnings
1928	$1,250.41	100.0	$761.89	100.0
4-'29 to 4-'30	734.52	58.7	423.52	55.6
4-'30 to 4-'31	678.07	54.2	453.09	59.5
4-'31 to 4-'32	557.00	44.6	385.73	50.6
Annual Average, 4-'29 to 4-'32	*656.53*	*52.5*	*420.78*	*55.2*

TABLE 46

*Average Earnings per Annum of Those Working and Seeking Work for the Three-
Year Period 4-'29 to 4-'32*

(Expressed as amounts and percentages of 1928 earnings)

		MEN			WOMEN	
AGE GROUPS	Number Seeking Work	AVERAGE ANNUAL EARNINGS		Number Seeking Work	AVERAGE ANNUAL EARNINGS	
		Amount per Annum 4-'29 to 4-'32	Per Cent of 1928 Earnings		Amount per Annum 4-'29 to 4-'32	Per Cent of 1928 Earnings
15–19	17	$588.46	101.6	50	$457.27	77.3
20–24	14	559.37	49.7	36	491.21	59.0
25–29	18	589.26	43.8	43	419.57	52.2
30–34	23	949.62	66.3	15	464.74	51.5
35–39	15	835.69	59.7	23	272.40	31.3
40–44	27	736.73	53.8	18	392.37	52.7
45–49	15	654.37	50.5	12	468.16	57.3
50–54	11	384.97	28.6	5	262.55	39.6
55–59	12	386.33	27.3	2	10.29	1.7
60–64	5	308.05	32.7	0	.....	...
65–69	1	794.56	93.9	0	.....	...
70–74	0	.....	...	0	.....	...
Average	158	$656.53	52.5	204	$420.78	55.2

TABLE 47

Comparative Records of Skilled, Semi-skilled, and Unskilled Workers (Men)

A. Average period unemployed for each of three years, 4-'29 to 4-'32, Represented
as Months and Per Cent of Total Time

		EXTENT OF UNEMPLOYMENT					
DEGREE OF SKILL	Number Working or Seeking Work	4-'29 to 4-'30		4-'30 to 4-'31		4-'31 to 4-'32	
		Months Unemployed	Per Cent of Total Time	Months Unemployed	Per Cent of Total Time	Months Unemployed	Per Cent of Total Time
Skilled	48	4.8	39.9	4.4	36.9	5.3	43.9
Semi-skilled	70	3.8	31.3	3.6	30.4	4.5	37.7
Unskilled	40	4.6	37.6	4.0	33.5	4.8	40.3

B. Average earnings for 1928 and each of three years, 4-'29 to 4-'32

DEGREE OF SKILL	Number Working or Seeking Work	AVERAGE EARNINGS			
		1928	4-'29 to 4-'30	4-'30 to 4-'31	4-'31 to 4-'32
Skilled	48	$1,394.39	$696.98	$708.82	$505.34
Semi-skilled	70	1,270.26	808.41	688.78	602.54
Unskilled	40	1,042.88	650.25	622.42	539.30

C. Earnings for each of three years, 4-'29 to 4-'32, represented as per cent
of 1928 earnings

DEGREE OF SKILL	Number Working or Seeking Work	PER CENT OF 1928 EARNINGS		
		4-'29 to 4-'30	4-'30 to 4-'31	4-'31 to 4-'32
Skilled	48	50.0	50.8	36.2
Semi-skilled...........	70	63.6	54.2	47.4
Unskilled	40	62.3	59.7	51.7

TABLE 48

Comparative Records of Skilled, Semi-skilled, and Unskilled Workers (Women)

A. Average period unemployed for each of three years, 4-'29 to 4-'32, represented as months and per cent of working time

DEGREE OF SKILL	Number Working or Seeking Work	EXTENT OF UNEMPLOYMENT					
		4-'29 to 4-'30		4-'30 to 4-'31		4-'31 to 4-'32	
		Months Unemployed	Per Cent of Total Time	Months Unemployed	Per Cent of Total Time	Months Unemployed	Per Cent of Total Time
Skilled	136	4.7	39.0	3.8	31.6	3.8	31.3
Semi-skilled ...	49	4.5	37.8	2.9	24.9	3.7	30.4
Unskilled	19	5.3	44.3	2.8	23.6	3.9	33.1

B. Average earnings for 1928 and for each of three years, 4-'29 to 4-'32

DEGREE OF SKILL	Number Working or Seeking Work	AVERAGE EARNINGS			
		1928	4-'29 to 4-'30	4-'30 to 4-'31	4-'31 to 4-'32
Skilled	136	$783.55	$408.05	$424.78	$386.66
Semi-skilled	49	748.13	469.83	522.69	374.51
Unskilled	19	642.33	414.89	476.19	407.93

C. Earnings for each of three years, 4-'29 to 4-'32, represented as per cent of 1928 earnings

DEGREE OF SKILL	Number Working or Seeking Work	PER CENT OF 1928 EARNINGS		
		4-'29 to 4-'30	4-'30 to 4-'31	4-'31 to 4-'32
Skilled	136	52.1	54.2	49.3
Semi-skilled	49	62.8	69.9	50.1
Unskilled	19	64.6	74.1	63.5

TABLE 49

Change in Industrial Status (Men)

STATUS OF LAST JOB	STATUS WITH L. CANDEE COMPANY			Total
	Skilled	Semi-skilled	Unskilled	
Skilled	8	8	2	18
Semi-skilled	8	12	7	27
Unskilled	32	50	31	113
Total	48	70	40	158

TABLE 50

*Per Cent of Male Workers Classified as Skilled, Semi-skilled, and Unskilled,
L. Candee Job and Last Job*

JOB	Per Cent Skilled	Per Cent Semi-skilled	Per Cent Unskilled
L. Candee Job....................	30.4	44.3	25.3
Last Job	11.4	17.1	71.5

TABLE 51—A

Annual Earnings of All Age Groups for 1928 and for Each of Three Years*
4-'29 to 4-'32

	NUMBER IN ALL AGE GROUPS	EARNINGS IN EACH YEAR			
		1928	4-'29 to 4-'30	4-'30 to 4-'31	4-'31 to 4-'32
Men	158	$197,564.35	$116,053.63	$107,134.71	$88,005.72
Women	204	155,424.71	86,398.73	92,429.71	78,688.62
Total	362	$352,989.06	$202,452.36	$199,564.42	$166,694.34

* Incomes for only those workers for whom schedules were obtained in the 1932
survey are included in these tables.

TABLE 51—B

Loss in Earnings of All Age Groups for Each of the Three Years, 4-'29 to 4-'32*
(Difference between 1928 income and that of each of three years)

	NUMBER IN ALL AGE GROUPS	LOSS IN EARNINGS FOR EACH YEAR		
		4-'29 to 4-'30	4-'30 to 4-'31	4-'31 to 4-'32
Men	158	$81,510.72	$90,429.64	$109,558.63
Women	204	69,025.98	62,995.00	76,736.09
Total	362	$150,536.70	$153,424.64	$186,294.72

* Incomes for only those workers for whom schedules were obtained in the 1932
survey are included in these tables.

TABLE 52

Number and Per Cent of Those Seeking Work Unemployed at Beginning of Each Month, 4-'29 to 3-'32

YEAR AND MONTH	NUMBER UNEMPLOYED ON FIRST OF EACH MONTH		PER CENT UNEMPLOYED ON FIRST OF EACH MONTH	
	Men 158	Women 204	Men 158	Women 204
1929				
April (6)	109	144	69.0	70.6
May	78	105	49.4	51.5
June	63	89	39.9	43.6
July	55	81	34.8	39.7
August	50	80	31.7	39.2
September	51	74	32.3	36.3
October	46	69	29.1	33.8
November	45	58	28.5	28.4
December	46	71	29.1	34.8
1930				
January	41	71	26.0	34.8
February	42	64	26.6	31.4
March	49	58	31.0	28.4
April	46	58	29.1	28.4
May	50	57	31.7	27.9
June	48	56	30.4	27.5
July	50	62	31.7	30.4
August	53	65	33.5	31.9
September	51	59	32.3	28.9
October	48	55	30.4	27.0
November	54	54	34.2	26.5
December	54	58	34.2	28.4
1931				
January	58	59	36.7	28.9
February	57	65	36.1	31.9
March	58	68	36.7	33.3
April	56	63	35.4	30.9
May	60	62	38.0	30.4
June	61	65	38.6	31.9
July	60	66	38.0	32.4
August	59	68	37.3	33.3
September	59	61	37.3	29.9
October	61	58	38.6	28.4
November	62	63	39.2	30.9
December	69	65	43.7	31.9
1932				
January	71	69	44.9	33.8
February	72	61	45.6	29.9
March	72	63	45.6	30.9

TABLE 53

Cumulative Effects of Unemployment

(Represented as Months Unemployed by Average Worker on the First Day of Months Indicated)

	May	June	July	Aug.	Sept.	Oct.	Nov.	Dec.	Jan.	Feb.	Mar.	Apr.
					5-'29 TO 4-'30							
Men	.4	1.2	1.7	1.9	2.2	2.5	2.8	3.1	3.4	3.7	3.9	4.3
Women	.4	1.2	1.6	2.0	2.4	2.8	3.1	3.4	3.8	4.1	4.4	4.7
					5-'30 TO 4-'31							
Men	4.6	4.9	5.2	5.5	5.8	6.2	6.5	6.8	7.2	7.5	7.9	8.2
Women	4.9	5.3	5.5	5.8	6.2	6.5	6.7	6.9	7.3	7.6	7.9	8.2
					5-'31 TO 4-'32							
Men	8.6	8.9	9.4	9.7	10.1	10.5	10.9	11.3	11.7	12.2	12.6	13.1
Women	8.5	8.8	9.2	9.5	9.8	10.1	10.4	10.7	11.0	11.4	11.7	11.9

TABLE 54—A.

Number of Families Receiving Aid for First Time at Various Periods

	NUMBER OF FAMILIES RECEIVING AID				
SOURCE OF AID	Before April, 1929	After April, 1929	Within 1st Year	Within 2nd Year	Within 3rd Year
Private	15	14	3	5	6
Public	36	33	5	17	11
Citizens Com. on Empl.	0	53	1	22	30
Total	51	100	9	44	47

TABLE 54—B.

Distribution of Families Receiving Aid

	NUMBER OF FAMILIES RECEIVING AID				
	Dept. of Public Charities	Citizen's Committee on Employment	State Aid for Widows	Private Agency No. 1	Private Agency No. 2
Assisted by organization alone	27	44	1	5	2
Assisted in coöperation with other organizations	65	47	3	43	15
Total	92	91	4	48	17

TABLE 54–C.

Expenditures for Relief of Former L. Candee Workers by Public and Private Agencies (4-'29 to 4-'32)

	EXPENDITURES BY PUBLIC AGENCIES					EXPENDITURES BY PRIVATE AGENCIES				Grand Total of Public and Private Aid
	Citizen's Committee on Employment	Dept. of Public Charities	State Aid for Widows	Total Public Aid	% of Grand Total	Private Agency No. 1	Private Agency No. 2	Total Private Aid	% of Grand Total	
4-29 to 4-30......	$ 42.00*	$1,953.95**	$1,065.09	$ 3,061.04	89.7	$ 156.48	$194.78	$ 351.26	10.3	$ 8,412.30
4-30 to 4-31......	1,197.00	1,494.03	551.00	3,242.03	72.5	844.13	384.92	1,229.05	27.5	4,471.08
4-31 to 4-32......	6,322.50	3,972.09	536.95	10,831.54	81.3	1,694.54	801.99	2,496.53	18.7	13,328.07

* The Citizen's Committee on Employment did not begin registering applicants until December, 1929.

** $1,160 was given to one family, the head of which was in the hospital several months.

TABLE 54—D.

Amount of Charity Received from All Agencies by Employes of L. Candee and Company
April, 1913 to April, 1932.

Year	Amount Received
4-1913 to 4-1914	$9.00
4-1914 to 4-1915	449.45
4-1915 to 4-1916	1,105.50
4-1916 to 4-1917	127.55
4-1917 to 4-1918	317.33
4-1918 to 4-1919	866.22
4-1919 to 4-1920	159.35
4-1920 to 4-1921	77.00
4-1921 to 4-1922	1,847.07
4-1922 to 4-1923	2,500.22
4-1923 to 4-1924	5.63
4-1924 to 4-1925	4,035.11
4-1925 to 4-1926	22.15
4-1926 to 4-1927	1,433.41
4-1927 to 4-1928	424.84
4-1928 to 4-1929	117.23
4-1929 to 4-1930	3,412.30
4-1930 to 4-1931	4,471.08
4-1931 to 4-1932	13,328.07
Grand Total	$34,708.71

TABLE 55

Average Months Unemployed, Employed in Sewing Trades, and Employed in Other
Jobs in Each Year, and Yearly Average for the Three-Year
Period, 4-'29 to 4-'32 (Women)

Age Groups	Number Working or Seeking Work	Unemployed				Sewing Trades				Other Jobs			
		4-'29 to 4-'30	4-'30 to 4-'31	4-'31 to 4-'32	3 Yrs. Average	4-'29 to 4-'30	4-'30 to 4-'31	4-'31 to 4-'32	3 Yrs. Average	4-'29 to 4-'30	4-'30 to 4-'31	4-'31 to 4-'32	3 Yrs. Average
15–19	50	3.4	2.7	3.1	3.1	1.7	3.2	4.3	3.1	6.9	6.1	4.7	5.9
20–24	36	3.9	2.4	3.8	3.4	2.8	3.4	3.4	3.2	5.3	6.3	4.8	5.4
25–29	43	4.7	3.3	3.2	3.7	2.1	2.8	2.9	2.6	5.2	5.9	5.9	5.7
30–34	15	6.4	4.5	3.9	4.9	1.7	3.4	4.0	3.0	3.9	4.1	4.1	4.0
35–39	23	6.7	5.4	6.2	6.1	1.2	2.7	2.5	2.1	4.1	3.9	3.3	3.8
40–44	18	6.1	4.3	3.7	4.7	1.2	1.2	1.6	1.3	4.7	6.6	6.8	6.0
45–49	12	3.2	1.7	1.8	2.2	1.9	2.3	2.8	2.3	6.9	8.1	7.4	7.5
50–54	5	5.1	7.6	5.0	5.9	.3	...	...	.1	6.6	4.4	7.0	6.0
55–59	2	11.6	12.0	12.0	11.9	...	...	...	...	.4	...	...	.1
Average	204	4.7	3.5	3.8	3.9	1.9	2.8	3.1	2.6	5.4	5.7	5.1	5.4

TABLE 56

Per Cent of Time Unemployed, Employed in Sewing Trades, and Employed in Other Jobs (Women)

AGE GROUPS	NUMBER WORKING OR SEEKING WORK	PER CENT OF TOTAL TIME											
		UNEMPLOYED				SEWING TRADES				OTHER JOBS			
		4-'29 to 4-'30	4-'30 to 4-'31	4-'31 to 4-'32	3 Yrs. Aver-age	4-'29 to 4-'30	4-'30 to 4-'31	4-'31 to 4-'32	3 Yrs. Aver-age	4-'29 to 4-'30	4-'30 to 4-'31	4-'31 to 4-'32	3 Yrs. Aver-age
15–19	50	28.1	22.8	25.6	25.5	14.3	26.4	35.5	25.4	57.6	50.8	38.9	49.1
20–24	36	32.6	19.9	31.6	28.1	23.6	28.0	28.2	26.6	43.8	52.1	40.2	45.3
25–29	43	39.3	27.7	26.5	31.2	17.8	23.5	24.0	21.8	42.9	48.8	49.5	47.1
30–34	15	53.1	37.8	32.8	41.2	14.2	28.3	33.3	25.3	32.8	33.9	33.9	33.5
35–39	23	56.2	44.8	51.5	50.8	9.8	22.8	21.0	17.9	34.1	32.4	27.5	31.3
40–44	18	51.0	35.7	30.6	39.1	10.2	9.7	12.9	10.9	38.8	54.6	56.5	49.9
45–49	12	26.2	13.9	15.3	18.5	16.3	18.8	22.9	19.3	57.5	67.4	61.8	62.2
50–54	5	42.5	63.3	41.7	49.2	2.5	...	...	.8	55.0	36.7	58.3	50.0
55–59	2	96.9	100.0	100.0	98.9	...	...	...	...	3.1	...	...	1.0
Average	204	39.2	29.3	31.3	33.2	15.5	22.9	26.1	21.5	45.3	47.7	42.7	45.3

TABLE 57

Weekly Wages—Sewing Trades and Other Jobs for Three One-Year Periods, 4-'29 to 4-'32 (Women)

AGE GROUPS	WEEKLY WAGES					
	SEWING TRADES			OTHER JOBS		
	4-'29 to 4-'30	4-'30 to 4-'31	4-'31 to 4-'32	4-'29 to 4-'30	4-'30 to 4-'31	4-'31 to 4-'32
15–19.........	$10.78	$9.18	$8.83	$14.14	$13.29	$11.34
20–24.........	13.61	11.78	11.50	15.12	13.68	12.10
25–29.........	8.70	11.55	9.00	13.96	12.54	11.50
30–34.........	14.08	14.05	12.45	16.16	17.22	16.45
35–39.........	12.43	9.62	9.76	11.84	11.18	9.51
40–44.........	11.46	10.50	8.63	14.61	13.10	11.55
45–49.........	6.06	5.78	5.18	14.95	12.91	10.48
50–54.........	15.00	....	....	10.73	10.68	8.52
Average	$11.14	$10.63	$9.60	$14.17	$13.15	$11.53

TABLE 58

Comparison of Average Months Unemployed, Employed in Sewing Trades, Employed in Other Jobs, in Wards 10, 11, 12, and in All Other Districts (Women)

WORK CLASSI-FICATION	NUMBER WORKING OR SEEKING WORK	MONTHS UNEMPLOYED			
		4-'29 to 4-'30	4-'30 to 4-'31	4-'31 to 4-'32	Annual Average for 3 Years
Unemployed					
Wards 10, 11, and 12	59	3.2	2.3	3.3	2.9
Other districts	145	5.3	4.0	3.9	4.4
Sewing Trades					
Wards 10, 11, and 12	59	3.3	4.5	4.2	3.9
Other districts	145	1.3	2.1	2.7	2.0
Other Jobs					
Wards 10, 11, and 12	59	5.6	5.3	4.4	5.1
Other districts	145	5.4	5.9	5.4	5.6